A
GARDEN
MISCELLANY

For Joe

Published in 2019 by Timber Press, Inc.
The Haseltine Building
133 S.W. Second Avenue, Suite 450
Portland, OR 97204-3527

timberpress.com

Printed in China
Cover and interior illustrations by Julia Yellow
Text and cover design by Adrianna Sutton

ISBN 978-1-60469-881-7
Catalog records for this book are available from
the Library of Congress and the British Library.

FSC
www.fsc.org
MIX
Paper from
responsible sources
FSC® C014688

A GARDEN MISCELLANY

An Illustrated Guide *to the* Elements *of the* Garden

Suzanne
STAUBACH

Illustrated by **JULIA YELLOW**

TIMBER PRESS • PORTLAND, OR

Contents

Introduction

If gardens were musical compositions, this book would be a look at the notes. Gardens have many notes, many parts. Paths, borders, beds, containers, pergolas, plants. Not all gardens, of course, include the same elements, but they do include some combination.

Gardens separated by millennia share remarkable similarities. My son sits with my granddaughters in the leafy shade of their grape arbor on a hot day, much as an Egyptian family sat under their grape arbor thousands of years ago. My cottage garden is a space of curves, but in the front, I have four beds in the universal quadripartite layout going back to the time of Cyrus the Great, circa sixth century BCE. Interpretations of each element vary in time and place and with individual gardeners, but the likenesses are strong.

With the benefit of world travel and interconnectivity, we can create gardens in styles from distant lands or times. Often, a specialty garden is part of a larger garden. Thus, within the greater landscape, we can incorporate a rock garden or a Japanese garden, so I count those sub-gardens also as elements.

There is much to discover in gardening. There is enough information, enough to learn, that each chapter of this book could be its own book. I have tried to distill the stories to their essence, to the anatomy underlying the gardens we visit and the gardens we make.

As I wrote, I wanted to add everything to my own garden. Oh, for a pond! Or a shepherd's hut! For a week, I thought nothing would do but a pavilion. Gardening is dreaming.

Enjoy!

Suzanne (Suzy) Staubach
Willow Tree Pottery, Ashford, Connecticut

Allée

Derived from *aller*, the French verb meaning to go, allée refers to a straight walkway or avenue, a promenade, usually lined with trees, occasionally with shrubs. Allées lead the garden visitor from a specific place, such as the entrance of a house, to a feature, such as a fountain or statue. The avenue can connect two gardens, serve as the drive to an estate, or guide movement through a park.

An allée can be the main axis of the garden, or sited elsewhere. In most cases, it is bordered on both sides by a single variety of tree or shrub. Specimens should be precisely and evenly planted in two rows, each plant directly opposite the plant on the other side of the allée. To be successful, measurements between the trees should be exact. Allées can have the illusion of greater length if the path is narrowed at the destination end and the trees are grown at descending heights. This is particularly useful for small formal gardens. As always in horticulture, and especially with an allée, one must take into account the size of the trees at maturity.

André Le Nôtre, gardener to Louis XIV (the Sun King) is credited with popularizing the allée and forever associating it with French gardens, though other designers were working in the same idiom at the time. Le Nôtre designed the spare-no-expense gardens at Versailles, which were meant to show off the king's wealth and power. Versailles was also designed to keep the nobles where the king could watch over them and hold their power in check. Strolling the magnificent allées that stretched across the gardens became a fashionable way for these men and women of the court to see and be seen. Le Nôtre's work at Versailles was inspired by the Italian Renaissance allées, lined with slim cypress trees. These in turn were, perhaps, inspired by the allées of the ancient Persians.

The seventeenth-century diarist, author, and gardener John Evelyn, writing in *Elysium Britannicum, or The Royal Gardens* (his magnum opus, a never-finished book of advice for gardeners), admonished that "alleys" must not be interrupted, as they "do with their length alone afford a most gracious and pleasant perspective, whilst they serve to decline and concur in a point, especially if planted with (tall) trees, then which nothing can be more ravishing and agreeable." Who would not want a garden element that is "ravishing and agreeable"?

Edith Wharton's allée at her Berkshire home, The Mount, is classic in execution and relies heavily on structure. The lime walkway of pleached European linden trees connects two gardens: the colorful French Flower Garden and the sunken Italian Garden. It runs north to south, parallel to her house rather than from it, and is overlooked by her balustraded terrace. Pleached trees are planted in a line and the branches are pruned and woven together, creating a sort of hedge. These trees provided shade for Wharton's guests, and add a strong note of formality.

Allées can have the illusion of greater length if the path is narrowed at the destination end and the trees are grown at descending heights.

Many different trees can be used to create an allée: hawthorn, linden, laburnum, and hornbeam are traditional; oak, beech, and maples are stately and fitting for long drives and promenades; slim white birch can be used for airiness. Allées can be made of fastigiate or columnar varieties of trees. Shrubs such as yew, rhododendrons, or hydrangea are also successful.

Allée

12

These trees and shrubs can be pleached; clipped into cubes, balls, or pyramids; allowed to grow together over the allée to form a tunnel; or grown to great girth and height. Deciduous species work best if you want to form a tunnel. The late English garden designer and writer Rosemary Verey famously used yellow laburnum trees underplanted with purple allium for her allée at Barnsley House in the Cotswolds.

Careful consideration should be given to the surface of the allée. Shade and foot traffic make a lawn path difficult. Brick, stones, pavers, gravel, and bark mulch all work well. Since you are planting in shade thick with tree roots, underplant with species that will thrive in such conditions: small bulbs, ground covers, and shallow-rooted plants such as vinca.

Because they require considerable maintenance if clipped or pleached, as well as extensive space, allées are most often seen in great formal gardens and parks of generous acreage, supported by trained staff and adequate funds. However, with imagination and a careful choice of trees or shrubs, allées can enhance small gardens, too. A fieldstone path with a dozen or so plants of panicle hydrangea 'Limelight' underplanted with catmint or vinca minor would be lovely.

Arbor

An arbor is a freestanding structure for growing climbing plants, usually with two sides, sometimes three, and a top. There are typically four uprights, but arbors can be made with as few as two uprights or more than four. The front and back are open, unless there's a third side. The sides and top are often made of lath or lattice. Arbor tops can be flat, arched, or pointed. Sometimes there are facing benches on the sides, or if there are three sides, one bench on the back. An arbor offers a practical way to cultivate climbing and vining plants, but it also provides shade and, draped in blossoms and greenery, provides unsurpassed beauty in the garden.

Arbors are different from pergolas in that pergolas are more ornamental, structurally more substantial, and include a floor. A pergola can be treated as an arbor, but an arbor is not a pergola.

With roots in the Old French *erbier*, meaning grassy plot, meadow, or kitchen garden, and the Latin *arbor,* for tree, arbor evolved by the mid-fourteenth century to mean a shaded nook, a bower formed by intertwining trees, shrubs, or vines—likely because such edifices were so prevalent and had become synonymous with the space they inhabited.

The earliest depictions we have of arbors are from the ancient Egyptians, as early as the Old Kingdom 4000 years ago. Arbors then grew grapes, which were eaten fresh, dried for raisins, or made into wine. An early hieroglyph for both vineyard and wine is a stylized rendering of an arbor, consisting of two forked poles supporting a transom across the top, plump bunches of grapes hanging down, with a dangling bucket to suggest harvest. This charming grape arbor ideogram appears twice on the iconic Rosetta Stone. Middle Kingdom tomb images show grapevines trained into rounded bowers in the shape of an inverted bowl, so that the vines themselves form the arbor. Other images show an arbor constructed in the center of an orchard.

Though these arbors were for food production, the Egyptians also enjoyed the cool shade they provided, a welcome respite from their hot climate. The Romans, who liked to dine al fresco, were talented architects and garden designers and often included arbors in their courtyard gardens. Monastery and peasant gardens of the Middle Ages utilized arbors, as did the grand gardens of the Renaissance. "Right on into the New Period, vineyard arbours were the centre and chief ornament of all gardens," Marie-Luise Gothein writes in her comprehensive classic, *A History of Garden Art*.

By the nineteenth century in the United States and UK, arbors were ubiquitous, entering our collective imaginations. Planted with roses, honeysuckle, morning glories, trumpet vines, or clematis, they might mark an opening in a picket fence and perhaps include a gate. You could find them on a meandering garden path in the midst of hollyhocks and snapdragons or at one end of the vegetable garden. They were usually made of wood, but gardeners of the Victorian era who had the means often installed Gothic arbors with lavish embellishment. Grape arbors were a key element in the tiny but productive city gardens of newly arrived immigrants, particularly Italians who might also use arbors to grow their beloved giant cucuzza squash.

Arbors today are constructed in many styles and materials to suit various types of landscaping. Manufactured arbors can be made of wood, powdered metal, steel, wrought iron, and vinyl, but many gardeners opt to make their own or have one custom made. The structures are typically anchored in the ground to withstand harsh weather and the weight of the plants they often support.

Many arbors are sited in full sun because they produce some shade. They can be connected to the garden by fencing, a wall, hedges, a path, or borders on either side. The placement of an arbor has a significant effect on how a garden is navigated and viewed. It can encourage guests to stroll through to see what's on the other side. It can frame a view of an urn or statue. It can invite one to linger a moment and sit if there is a bench. An arbor can separate areas of the garden or define a space. Often, especially in a small garden, an arbor is the main focal point. In cold climates, a well-made arbor adds winter interest even after the leaves and flowers of the vines have disappeared. And, as professional photographers know, an arbor can add romance and magic to photos.

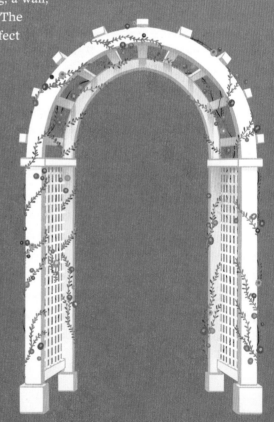

Arboretum

You could say an arboretum is a botanical garden of trees. It is a place for the scientific study and public exhibition of a collection of trees, or trees and shrubs. The collection can include natives, exotics, a combination of natives and exotics, or a particular grouping of trees, such as conifers or oaks. Arboretums are usually planted on large acreages—parks, campuses, private estates—but small properties can also be successfully planted with a tree collection.

Hatshepsut, the great female pharaoh of Egypt in the fifteenth century BCE, commissioned an expedition of five ships to sail south to Punt (believed to be present-day Somalia or Eritrea). Here, thirty-one frankincense trees were dug, shipped back in individual baskets, and planted at her palace. This is the first recorded instance of exotic trees being transplanted. Ancient Egyptians also collected exotic trees from Sudan and Syria for royal gardens. Other early peoples such as the Assyrians, Babylonians, and Romans collected trees.

We do not know for certain when the beautiful Trsteno Arboretum, on the Adriatic coast of Croatia, was begun, but records show that it was already flourishing by 1492. Legend tells us that the Gozze (Gučetić) family, a local clan of nobles, poets, artists, philosophers, and intellectuals, asked the seafarers who sailed from nearby Dubrovnik to bring back seeds from their travels to plant on the family's estate. Though this ancient arboretum has suffered grave losses of trees from wars, weather, and arson, it continues to thrive with over 200 specimens of Mediterranean and tropical trees that attract visitors from around the world.

> Besides being for leisure and enjoyment, an arboretum is usually for study, education, and often research.

The word arboretum, from the Latin *arbor*, came into usage in the nineteenth century. Some etymologists credit John Claudius Loudon, the eighteenth-century London-based gardener, writer, magazine publisher, and landscape designer, with coining it. Drawing upon his own master work published in 1838, *Arboretum et Fruticetum Britannicum*, he designed the Derby Arboretum in Derby, England, as a public park.

Loudon made planting mounds and serpentine paths, giving the Derby Arboretum a spacious and inviting feel. He collected 800 species of trees and shrubs, one of each, from around the world, then arranged them in the arboretum by their botanical family groups. He also produced a catalog of the trees and shrubs for visitors so they would know what they were looking at and could gain some botanical education.

Arboreta can be found throughout the world, including the National Arboretum in Washington, DC, Eastwoodhill Arboretum in New Zealand, Kew Gardens in London, and dozens more. Many were the beneficiaries of the plant hunters of the nineteenth and early twentieth centuries and were created to hold the bounty of their explorations.

The garden writer Allen Lacy devoted his later years to the tiny (less than an acre) Linwood Arboretum. Here he wanted to showcase trees and shrubs not usually planted by homeowners and inspire his neighbors to become a bit more adventuresome in their landscaping. He also wanted an arboretum that was frequently seen—it is in a busy part of town—and could be casually enjoyed by passersby. Linwood demonstrates how effective a small arboretum can be. Arboreta were a popular addition to estates during the Country House era, but we see from Lacy that it is possible to have an arboretum on a suburban plot.

Besides being for leisure and enjoyment, an arboretum is usually for study, education, and often research. This requires design considerations that do not apply to other gardens, such as grouping by taxonomy, the necessity of labels, and the need to allow enough space between specimens for optimum growth conditions. Nevertheless, an arboretum is a garden for people, so aesthetic considerations and ease of movement are also important. This can lead to design tensions.

When the arboretum at Royal Botanic Gardens, Kew in the UK was being expanded and rejuvenated in the nineteenth century, director Sir William Hooker brought in the watercolorist-turned-landscape designer, William Andrews Nesfield, as the designer. Once Nesfield realized that the trees were to be displayed according to their taxonomical relationships, he had second thoughts about accepting the commission. Such strictures were an affront to his artistic landscape skills. Hooker, for his part, scoffed that Nesfield was too focused on geometry. Nevertheless, Nesfield came up with plans that were largely satisfactory to both, with sunken paths (invisible from a distance), planting mounds, glades, and three vistas. He was even able to include a shrub parterre as a nod to formal garden design.

Included in most arboreta are paths that invite visitors through and bring them close enough to individual specimen trees to see the bark and leaves and structure. Planting mounds, though not necessary, are popular. Some sort of identification signage is also important. Small aluminum signs with the common name and Latin name are often affixed to the trees. Maps are useful and fun.

Day to day, an arboretum is less labor intensive than a garden of herbaceous and mixed borders. It has four-season interest, with winter, especially in temperate climates, often the most dramatic time of year. Public arboreta are important resources for gardeners, scientists, and visitors. The appearance of pocket arboreta in small towns and neighborhoods is, happily, a growing trend.

Arboretum Time

Time is a factor in all gardens but especially in an arboretum. Trees take many years to reach their full height and girth. It is not uncommon for trees to live 150 years, with some species living many centuries. When you plant an arboretum, although you will be able to enjoy it yourself, you are planting for the future. But trees can be felled by disease, wind, lightning, fire, and heavy snows. The loss of a mature tree, or a number of mature trees, will leave gaping absences in the plan and can be emotionally upsetting for arborists and visitors alike. You cannot replace a giant white oak toppled by the winds of a hurricane as easily as a treasured daylily devoured by deer.

Arch

A weathered stone or brick arch, be it freestanding or incorporated into a wall, lends an air of antiquity to a landscape. It gives a sense of permanence and majesty. Long after a garden has reverted to brambles or forest, the arch will remain. A masonry arch is an element of classic proportions and beauty, as well as a symbol of strength. It draws the eye to look beyond, enticing the viewer to pass through to the other side. It is a place to pause and pose for a photo.

The arch shapes we most often encounter in gardens are wood or metal arbors, but here we will discuss the classic masonry arch, a marriage of physics and geometry. An arch is a curve that spans an opening. It can span greater expanses than a lintel and support more weight. Ancient Egyptians and Babylonians understood the arch, but it was the Romans who had a genius for the form and used it in their building projects—most famously their aqueducts, many of which still stand after two millennia.

The Roman arch or sprung arch can be rounded, somewhat flattened, or an inverted U. It exerts a downward and outward thrust and requires buttressing on the sides to keep it from collapsing. A Roman arch works well as an opening in a garden wall, with the wall acting as the buttress. Roman arches can be lined up next to each other, each serving as the buttress for the next, as with a portico. Roman arches are also used as niches in walls to hold an urn or shelter a bench, as the opening in an outdoor oven, or as the span of a stone bridge.

> It was the Romans who had a genius for the form and used it in their building projects—most famously their aqueducts.

The catenary arch (from the Latin word for chain, because it is described by tracing the arc of a chain which is suspended at two points, and then inverted) is self-supporting. It requires no buttressing. It is the simplest arch to build and exceedingly strong. Many consider it to be nature's most beautiful curve.

Most gardeners hire a professional mason if they want a stone or brick arch, but once the principles are understood, anyone, with care, can build one, especially a catenary arch. Wedge-shaped bricks and stones are commercially available, which simplifies the construction.

Arches are built on forms and rely on a keystone tightly fitted into the exact center of the top. Alternating stones or bricks are added to each side. When the two sides meet, this central, wedge-shaped keystone is added, locking the arch together. Once the keystone is in place the form is removed—always a dramatic moment. To spectators, it seems the arch will surely collapse.

There are talented masons who specialize in building stone arches. Artists also make ceramic or cement arches that are then tiled. Many large or elaborate arches are created as commissions, often for public gardens or as community projects. You can purchase ready-made arches, or "ruins" of arches. These include gothic designs with points at the top, like church windows. And on a lucky day, one can find an old arch at a salvage yard, ready to be brought home and reassembled.

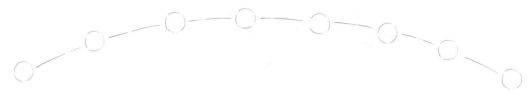

Aspect

When landscape designers speak of a garden's aspect, they are referring to the compass point it faces. A garden's aspect affects the amount and timing of the sun it receives and the direction shadows fall at various times of day. Aspect influences which plants will grow best. It also influences the time of day the garden can be most enjoyed. A garden with an eastern aspect would generally be sunniest in the morning. This would be a nice spot to drink your morning tea or coffee. Similarly, a garden with a western aspect would generally be sunny at the end of the day, pleasant for dining al fresco or after-work weeding. A garden with a southern aspect will generally have plenty of sun, and a garden with a northern aspect will likely be cool and shady.

Most houses are not sited on a strict aspect and might face south-southwest or north-northeast instead of directly north or south. A compass is helpful in determining your aspect. You will also want to observe where the sun rises and sets. It is important to track the shadows cast by the house, nearby buildings, and trees. Keep an hourly record of the sun and shade for a year. You might have a wonderful south-facing aspect, but surrounding large trees or tall buildings could prevent the sun from reaching your ground.

If your summers tend to be hot, you might prefer a garden with a northern aspect, though your plant palette will be more limited than with a south-facing yard. In the southern hemisphere, the principle is the same but the north and south conditions are reversed.

Whether you are deciding where to plant a garden, how to site a house to be built, whether or not to purchase a particular home, or how a garden will be used, the aspect of a home and its yard is one of a property's most important elements. It can influence how best to design, plant, and use the space.

Axis

An axis is the key element defining and organizing a formal garden. It is an imaginary line which orients and describes the space. The main axis often runs through the house, leading straight out into the gardens both front and back if the doors are aligned. It can lead out from a terrace, deck, or porch. An axis does not have to be a walk, but it often is. It can be a lawn or long terrace, or a series of enclosed lawns, with symmetrical plantings on both sides. To add interest, an axis can have stopping points. It can widen into a gravel circle planted with herbs. Three or four arbors planted with clematis and roses could be placed over an axis.

In addition to the main axis, there are usually cross axes leading to other parts of the garden and bound by additional gardens or features. Thus, with a main axis and secondary axes, the garden designer can create garden compartments, and direct movement through the garden. An axis defines the views from the house, and it can also be used to create internal vistas. It controls the experience of the garden. Because an axis is linear and predictable, it offers a sense of calm. The surprises—a statue at the end of the axis, parterres on each side of a cross axis, an opening in a hedge revealing a view—are created by the garden designer.

Land might slope away from the house, dip here and there, or rise to a higher point. To accommodate this change in terrain, you can add steps to your axis. This could be a place to set a few urns or flowerpots, and slow your visitors' pace. You can make a small sunken garden where the land dips, creating drama. But always, the axis is a straight line, laid out with logic internal to the space—the organizing principle from which all else in a formal garden flows.

An axis makes a small urban garden feel larger and more spacious than one designed as a single space. It pulls one out of the house and into the garden.

> Because an axis is linear and predictable, it offers a sense of calm.

Balcony Garden

Balconies are an extension of an interior upper floor supported by corbels, brackets, or supports made of concrete, wood, or steel. They are enclosed by a waist-high metal railing, balustrades, or a wall. They may or may not have a roof. A gallery is similar to a balcony, but is supported from the ground level. It can be larger than a balcony and often stretches across one entire side of a building. A gallery can be on a ground floor, with one or two balconies above.

Architectural historians believe balconies were first built by the ancient Greeks to enhance the ventilation of their houses. Romans adopted them, too. During the Middle Ages, sturdy, roofed balconies were attached to fortresses during battle. They also became stylish additions to European residences.

In the late sixteenth century, Shakespeare romanticized balconies in his play *Romeo and Juliet*. Today, faux balconies constructed outside windows are called Juliet balconies.

One of the most famous balconies is the one at St. Peter's Basilica in the Vatican, where the Pope steps out and gives his blessing to the crowds below. Similarly, balconies encircle Islamic minarets from which the Islamic faithful are called to prayer. Carved wooden balconies draped with ivy geraniums are a defining feature of widely photographed Swiss chalets. Originating in the German, Swiss, and French Alps, they were copied in England and France, with many features appearing in houses of the Arts and Crafts Movement. A-frames, which became popular during the second-house movement of the 1950s and 1960s, were sometimes dressed up as faux chalets with balconies.

Perhaps the most iconic balconies are those of Paris, France, and of the French Quarter in New Orleans. Enclosed by lacy, wrought iron railings, they are festooned with bright flowers, often scarlet geraniums (pelargoniums), begonias, roses, or bougainvillea planted in pots and window boxes. Today, many multistory apartment buildings throughout the world feature private balconies for residents.

Balconies and galleries have unique aesthetic considerations. A balcony garden is designed to be seen from within the house or apartment. The plants and furniture must look inviting from the interior, drawing the visitor out. Thought must be given to the view from the balcony. Does it look down upon a private garden and if so, has that garden been designed for viewing from above? Are there distant mountain or ocean views? A skyline? Or does the balcony look out upon an ugly parking lot or congested city street that must be screened from view? Most balcony gardens are also meant to be looked at from below. While you may not want the strangers on the sidewalk to watch you sipping your morning coffee or watering your plants, you do want them to see the abundance of flowers and greenery within and spilling over the railing. Most important, the balcony garden is meant to be viewed from the balcony itself. If there is room, you will want a table and chairs where you can sit and read or enjoy a glass of wine. Thus, the balcony is viewed from within itself, from within the apartment or house, and from below.

Unlike an in-ground garden, you cannot plant a tree by digging a hole, amend the soil by dumping a truckload of compost, or use a wheelbarrow to scoot flats of seedlings to your balcony. All your plants must be grown in planters. Everything must be brought up and carried out. That means lugging heavy potting soil, pots, plants, furniture, and anything else you are going to add up flights of stairs or in an elevator and through the living space. In most instances, you will also have to carry water.

In the northern hemisphere, an unobstructed south facing balcony not only receives daylong sun, it can be a heat trap. Small pots dry out quickly, so it is prudent to have the largest pots or planters you can manage, keeping in mind that they also add weight. In the northern hemisphere, gardens with an east or west aspect get six to eight hours of sun; east provides morning sun and west, afternoon. However, even with a southern aspect, much of the sunlight can be blocked by nearby tall buildings. As with in-ground gardens, observation through the seasons is recommended.

A balcony with a north aspect will be a shade garden. This can be a challenge, but you won't get the extremes of temperatures and sun you get with the other aspects, nor will you have to water as often. Impatiens, ferns, coleus, caladiums, and fuchsia will thrive. North-facing balconies can be a nice spot for your houseplants to have a summer vacation.

A balcony garden, by virtue of its restricted size, is an outdoor room, an extension of the living quarters. It can be the entirety of the garden, or one room of a larger garden, offering in both instances an opportunity for beauty and sanctuary.

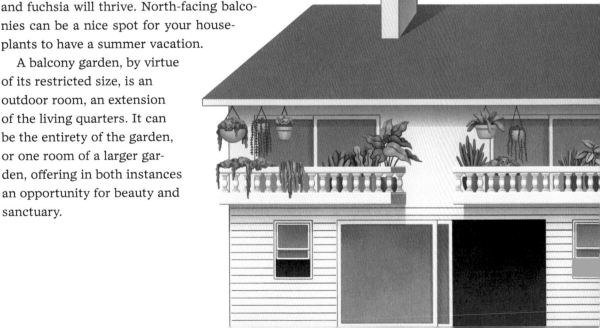

Bed

A garden bed is the ground where plants are grown. The word, originating from *bedd* in Old English, and before that the Proto-Germanic *badjam*, has long been associated with both a place to sleep or recline as well as a garden plot. The bed is the heart of a garden. Indeed, for some, the bed is the garden. Types of beds include dug beds, mounded beds and mounded rows, raised beds, waffle beds, sunken beds, and island beds.

A dug bed is dug directly into the ground. It can be an island, visible from all sides. It can be rectangular or curved. It can be a border, backed by a wall or hedge. Dug beds are found in traditional herb gardens, in the planting areas of parterres, and in a wide range of flower gardens.

Mounding is usually used for island beds. Amended topsoil is spread in a gentle mound on top of a dug bed, so that the center is the highest point, up to eight inches thick. A hoe or rake, or even your hands, work well for forming and shaping. Mounding adds to the bed's growing depth, enhances drainage, and increases plant visibility.

Types of beds include dug beds, mounded beds and mounded rows, raised beds, waffle beds, sunken beds, and island beds.

Vegetable gardens often rely on mounded rows. Here, soil is hoed up onto the planting rows, forming paths in between for easy access. The long, mounded beds created in this technique warm up a bit sooner than the surrounding plot and have good drainage.

Raised beds made with "boards or woven panels of willow" were recommended by the first-century Roman agricultural writer Columella, "to improve drainage for wetter regions, and for the cultivation of specific plants (garlic)." Later, the ninth-century German Benedictine abbot and poet Walafrid Strabo described using planks to make raised beds in monastery gardens. Indeed, raised beds were popular in the monastery gardens of the Middle Ages and beyond. They were also used in colonial America in the gardens kept close to the house by women.

Raised beds are essentially growing boxes constructed on the ground. They are usually between three and four feet across so the gardener can easily reach into the center from either side. They are typically six to eight feet long but can be any length the gardener wishes. The sides can be made of boards or woven panels of willow as Columella suggested, brick, cement blocks, rocks, or corrugated metal. They are usually one to two feet deep but can be made waist high for no-bend access, helpful for older and handicapped gardeners.

The soil in raised beds warms quickly in spring and drains well, which is beneficial for vegetable, herb, and cutting gardens. These beds are attractive and can be arranged in pleasant and practical geometric patterns. They are easy to tend.

A waffle bed is the opposite of a raised bed and best for arid climates. Here, the goal is to aid in irrigation and give the plants a bit of shelter. Waffle beds have been used for thousands of years by peoples as diverse as the ancient Egyptians and Native Americans in the U.S. Southwest. Suitable for deserts, they are also useful for areas where one wants to conserve water. The growing area is sunken.

A waffle bed is made by laying out a grid of squares. Each square is dug out. The removed earth is used to create berms around each square. More durable berms can also be made of clay. Waffles that are maintained can be used for years.

To water, the waffle bed is flooded so that water pools in the sunken area where it is retained, slowly sinking down to the roots. Contemporary waffle gardeners often incorporate drip systems.

Like waffle gardens, sunken beds conserve water and are usually made in warm, arid climates. They can be square, rectangular, circular, or free-form island beds. Sunken beds can also be used for borders. Here, the turf is removed and the bed excavated a foot in depth. Stones and roots are removed. The soil is set aside on a tarp and amended. The bed is then excavated again an additional six inches to a foot. The top amended layer is added back into the bed and smoothed, so that the bed is six inches to a foot below ground level. It should be thoroughly watered and allowed to settle before planting. These can be used for vegetables but more often are used for decorative gardens.

Island Beds

An island bed is meant to be viewed from all sides. It can be any shape—round, oval, crescent, square, kidney-shaped, or something irregular. Island beds are usually mounded above the surrounding landscape. The earth can be sculpted to place the highest point in the center or it can be sculpted asymmetrically. An island bed can also be built around an existing feature such as a tree or boulder.

Popular with Victorians for their colorful bedding schemes, island beds fell out of favor as gardeners turned to herbaceous borders. In the 1930s, round beds were made in suburban lawns and referred to simply as flower gardens, but serious gardeners continued to prefer borders.

In the 1950s, Alan Bloom caused a horticultural revolution when he made a display garden of multiple island beds planted with perennials at his famous nursery, Blooms of Bressingham. A prolific British author and nurseryman with an international following, he began with one island bed as a test. He had neglected staking his borders and while thinking about the nuisance of staking, it occurred to him that the perennials he grew in rows for his nursery stock did not need staking. Perhaps, he thought, it was the fact that borders had walls or hedges as backing that led to less sturdy plants. After a few years of testing, he concluded that perennials would perform better in the conditions an island bed offered than a border, with more available air and light and easy accessibility for maintenance.

Bloom expanded to forty-eight islands, creating a six-acre "dell garden" on his 200-acre nursery. He popularized the concept in his book, *Perennials in Island Beds*, in lectures, and at his nursery. Much photographed and visited, Bloom's island beds are now under the care of his son-in-law at the nursery, which continues under the care of his son, author Adrian Bloom.

Bloom-inspired island beds place taller plants in the center. Professional designers recommend that the height of the tallest perennials equal half the width of the bed, calling for an eight-foot-wide bed to have four-foot-tall plants in the center. Broad-leaved perennials are used around the edges to contrast with surrounding lawn. In between are medium-sized plants. Beds deeper than eight feet might have a path or stepping stones for access. Plants sturdy enough not to require staking are usually chosen, as supports are difficult to disguise. Each bed can have its own color scheme.

Nurserywoman, gardener, lecturer, and author Beth Chatto created island beds in the highly original and now-famous gravel garden she made in her dusty old car park. An advocate of placing the right plant in the right place, Chatto designed the gravel garden so that it would never need to be irrigated, yet the plants would thrive. She laid out the beds using garden hoses as outlines, rearranging them until she was pleased. Once that was achieved and the plants were established, she banished hoses from the gravel garden and relied solely on water from rainfall.

Island beds work well in both large and small gardens. You can have one island bed as a centerpiece or multiple island beds with wide swaths of lawn in between. You can place one in the center of a circular drive or remove some pavers to make one in a patio.

In addition to herbaceous plantings, and of course bedding (see next element entry), island beds can include a mix of bulbs, shrubs, small trees, annuals, and perennials. And in addition to being surrounded by lawn, they can also be placed in gravel or bark mulch. Offering gardeners freedom and opportunity, these oases of plantings are now an important addition to the designer's toolkit, and many gardens are a combination of island beds and borders.

Bedding, Carpet Bedding

The daring exploits of international plant hunters brought a stream of exotic plants to Victorian England and, shortly after, to Civil War–era America. Mid-nineteenth-century gardeners were besotted with the bold colors and new availability of these half-hardy perennials arriving by ship from South and Central America and South Africa. The end of the glass tax in England plus technical advances in greenhouse construction made it possible for temperate-zone gardeners to propagate such plants from hotter climes under glass, so that they could transplant them outdoors when cold winter temperatures abated.

To best show off these plants, the head gardeners of wealthier British citizens decided to arrange their gardens as blocks of color to maximize the impact. Soon, gardeners at the botanical gardens, particularly Kew and at public parks, were doing the same. There might be a mass of red pelargoniums planted next to a mass of yellow pocketbook plants from Chile. No intermingling allowed! Later, Victorian gardeners included brightly colored annuals as bedding plants, and more subtly, foliage plants.

Garden beds might be mounded island beds visible from all sides with the tallest plants in the center, but with all plants fairly short. The outlines of these beds could be round, oval, or kidney-shaped. The beds could be long serpentines or ruler-straight ribbons planted in stripes of various hues. They might be planted in geometric designs made of contrasting colors, much like the designs on drawing room carpets, hence the name carpet bedding. Gardeners began infilling parterres with bedding plants.

> There might be a mass of red pelargoniums planted next to a mass of yellow pocketbook plants.

For the main bedding garden at Linton, in Maidstone, England, John Robson, the head gardener and a frequent contributor to garden magazines, used thousands of Trentham rose geraniums, alyssum, lobelia, lady's purse, and the pelargonium cultivar 'General Tom Thumb' for his 1861 planting scheme. His bedding design was a large red flower outlined in white and set against a light blue background. Outside this he made spheres of orange, also in a blue background, and rimmed the whole in red. One visitor compared it to a Rubens painting.

Thousands of plants were required for bedding schemes. Anthony Huxley writes in his *Illustrated History of Gardening*, "In 1875 one two-acre south London garden is recorded as being bedded with 60,000 foliage plants of seventeen kinds."

A flourishing nursery business rose up to supply these unheard-of quantities of plants, particularly for those who did not have enough conservatory space to start so many thousands of plants themselves. Potters were busy throwing many tons of clay for seed pans and flowerpots to satisfy the market.

Bedding is expensive and labor intensive. In addition to planting three and sometimes four times in a season, beds must be deadheaded daily, watered, and weeded. When plants die or straggle, they have to replaced immediately lest the gap ruin the entire design.

With the onset of World War I, skilled labor became less available as men were called to fight. To compensate, gardeners turned to somewhat easier plants such as sedums, at least for the edges of the gardens. Other gardeners used bedding in only the most visible areas of their property, or those spaces seen from the windows of the house, then supplemented with mixed borders or shrubs for less-obvious areas.

It became increasingly difficult to afford the practice both financially and in terms of labor. And then, Gertrude Jekyll and William Robinson (both were garden designers and authors; Robinson was the publisher of a magazine to which they both contributed) initiated a horticultural rebellion against the stiff formality of bedding. They advocated for looser plantings. Robinson championed what he called the wild garden. Jekyll developed carefully orchestrated herbaceous and mixed borders. Generations of gardeners to this day follow their lead.

A derivative and simpler form of bedding appeared in suburbia during the mid-twentieth century and continues today. Examples are a fringe of massed impatiens along a house foundation or a bed planted entirely with zinnias or cosmos. And because of the reliable impact, some parks departments have continued to embrace bedding in at least a portion of their gardens. Bedding is also used in the meridians of roads and avenues. And of course, it is very appropriate for historically restored houses.

Happily, today's plants are improved from their Victorian counterparts, need far less care, and are not as fussy. It is not necessary to replant three or four times a year, as species that flower nonstop are plentiful. Some plants, such as wave petunias, do not need deadheading and thrive with nothing more than sunshine, water, and occasional fertilizer, unlike the demanding petunias during the bedding craze. Flats of annuals and tender perennials are readily available and modestly priced. Nor does one need a conservatory or greenhouse—it is not necessary to start plants from seed (though it is certainly possible). Bedding schemes are much easier to plant and maintain than they were at the height of bedding's popularity. Our Victorian forebears would be envious.

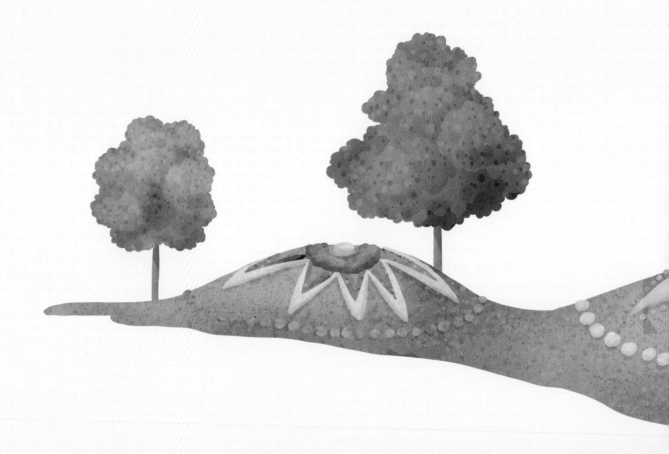

Bee Skep, Beehive

Gardeners of early civilizations sought to attract and keep bees, for their honey and wax, and also for the benefit of plants, once the crucial role of bees as pollinators was understood. Egyptians, Greeks, and Romans all kept bees, sometimes in old logs or baskets, but often in fired or unfired clay hives. Early American and British potters made terra-cotta hives, usually in dome shapes.

Colonial-era gardeners made inexpensive hives, called bee skeps by coiling straw to form domed cloche-like baskets. Though a well-made skep could last many years, the bees were harmed or killed while harvesting the honey and wax, and there was no way to open the skep and treat the bees for pests such as mites. Today, though no longer used in bee keeping, skeps are widely used as decoration in herb gardens.

In 1850, Lorenzo Langstroth invented a wood beehive with movable frames, which meant the honey and wax could be harvested without smoking the bees out or killing them. Many improvements have been made since, including insulation, but hives based on Langstroth's invention remain the most popular in the United States and Australia.

These wood beehives are customarily painted white. Set in an orchard or a quiet corner of a flower garden, their clean, simple lines fit nicely with informal and country gardens. They are also found in urban and rooftops gardens, even on the roof of Notre Dame in Paris. Gardeners who do not wish to keep bees themselves but want the benefits of pollination sometimes offer space for the hives of neighboring beekeepers.

Adventurous beekeepers paint their hives in bold primary colors or pastels—shades of reds, blues, yellows, even pinks and purples, with trim in contrasting bright shades. Rows of stacked, multicolored hives at the edge of a meadow make a bold and unforgettable statement and, it seems, delight the bees.

Birds

Gardeners have been attracting and keeping birds in their flower and pleasure gardens for millennia (even as their farming friends were shooing away what they considered feathered pests). Birds have been kept for their songs and their plumage, for their insect-eating benefits, and even for their guano.

As much as the birds themselves, the structures built to house them have become important and desirable elements of garden design. These include aviaries, dovecotes, chicken coops, chimney swift towers, birdhouses, and bird feeders.

The Sumerians had a word for birdcage, *subura*. Alexander the Great and his men captured parakeets in India in 526 BCE and brought them home in iron cages. The portico of the northern sunken garden of the desert palace built by Pharaoh Akhenaten and his wife, Nefertiti, was lined with niches believed to be used as nesting boxes for birds. Ancient Roman mosaics and frescoes depict lush garden scenes with numerous birds splashing in pools of water and flitting about the vines, potted plants, and shrubbery. Romans also built columbaria with numerous interior compartments to house their carrier pigeons.

The great Aztec leader Montezuma boasted a lavish aviary . . . filled with hundreds of birds.

In Turkey, by the fifteenth century, birdhouses were an important part of civic architecture, with simple birdhouses built into the walls of buildings. By the eighteenth century, birdhouses molded of concrete had become elaborate, decorative mini-palaces that protruded from the south-facing walls of important buildings. They are among the most beautiful birdhouses in the world.

Europeans also made birdhouses during the Middle Ages, particularly in Belgium and the Netherlands. Some were made of wood or basketry, but pottery birdhouses shaped like bottles or vases were more durable and prevailed. Early American potters also made bottle houses that could be attached to a house or barn. These were hand-thrown ceramic vessels, mounted horizontally. Prior to the Europeans' arrival in North America, Native Americans on the East Coast made birdhouses from hollowed-out chunks of birch.

In 1915, Althea Rosina Sherman built the first chimney swift tower, a charming structure with clapboard siding, a shingled hip roof, and a faux chimney. Inspired by Sherman, ornithologists and birders began constructing towers for swifts in backyards, parks, and gardens as a way to increase the swift population. Built of wood or masonry, surrounded by flowers, and low growing shrubs, they are a pretty addition to the landscape.

Aviaries have been garden features throughout history and throughout the world. The great Aztec leader Montezuma boasted a lavish aviary, decorated with latticework, gold, and jewels, and filled with hundreds of colorful birds, including parrots, macaws, and eagles. Aviaries appeared in China, in Germany during the Middle Ages, in Renaissance Italy, France, Spain, and later in English estates during the Country House era. Today public parks and zoos as well as large estates often include an aviary in the garden. Prefabricated "bird enclosures" (in essence, aviaries) fit well in a small garden.

Dovecotes (more prosaically, pigeon towers) are one of the most desirable bird-associated garden elements, as they are architecturally interesting. Arthur Cooke, who wrote *A Book of Dovecotes*, exclaimed that each dovecote was unique in "every detail, architectural style, shape, size, design of doorway, means of entrance for the inmates, number and arrangement of the nests." During the eighteenth cen-

tury, pigeon-keeping declined and many dovecotes stood empty and fell into disrepair. They were rediscovered by Gertrude Jekyll who appreciated good craftsmanship and design. She thought the old dovecotes were wonderful to look at and popularized them as garden features in her 1918 book, *Garden Ornament*. Today, dovecotes are a valued garden element, with or, more often, without birds. Many antique dovecotes have been restored and protected. Architects are designing new ones. Small wooden dovecotes, set atop poles, are readily available.

In recent years, there has been a resurgence of interest in keeping chickens in the home garden. Chickens require a chicken coop. Happily, today's chickens are not housed in the cheaply constructed, boxy affairs of yesterday. Coops have become the new dovecotes of the garden, serving as ornament and a vehicle for the gardener's creativity.

Birdhouses can decorate a garden of any size and type. Artisans create bird-houses that range from simple, rustic constructions to elaborate representations of churches, Victorian mansions, general stores, and more. A birdhouse can serve as a focal point in a garden, decorate a fence post or tree trunk, or reside on the side of a building. Just as you want your garden to suit the architecture of your house, you want your birdhouse to suit the style of your garden.

Today birdhouses are offered by ornithological specialists, big box stores, woodworkers, and artists. The gardener has a wealth of options to choose from.

Bird feeders are an even more prevalent addition to today's gardens than birdhouses. Like houses, they come in an array of designs from practical, squirrel-protected affairs to the more whimsical.

Bog Garden, Rain Garden

A bog is a wetland that, over time, has filled in with decayed plants. It consists of soft, water-logged ground. Bog gardens are planted in areas that are wet year-round, such as along the edges of natural or man-made ponds or bogs.

In the past, bogs, swamps, and marshes were considered useless, and often filled in to create dry land. Today we understand the importance of these soggy spaces to the environment. In many areas, such wetlands are protected.

A bog garden attracts wildlife such as dragonflies, frogs, toads, birds, and butterflies. It can support a rich array of plants that don't mind getting their feet wet, such as red chokecherry, shadblow serviceberry, sweet pepperbush, blue flag iris, and pickerel weed, to name a few.

Rain gardens are a relatively new idea. Developed in the 1990s to collect, absorb, and filter runoff water from roofs, roads, compacted lawns, paved areas, and other impervious surfaces, they have gained widespread adoption on college campuses, in residential developments, and in urban areas. They are an attractive solution to runoff in the private garden.

Gardeners construct rain gardens in both naturally occurring and artificial depressions, which they locate along a downward slope. The garden is sited at least ten feet away from the house or other buildings. Rain gardens do not work well in clay soils or over septic tanks.

Generally, six to twelve inches of soil are removed from the bottom of the depression and replaced with sand and compost, increasing the porosity. The garden is planted with shrubs and perennials that are often but not necessarily native to the region.

When it rains, the rain garden fills with water. However, within a day or two, the rainwater soaks into the ground, leaving the rain garden dry until another storm strikes. This is an attractive and cost-effective way to deal with runoff and can fit into most garden styles.

> Today we understand the importance of these soggy spaces to the environment.

Bones

One of the mistakes rookie gardeners often make is diving into the showy stuff first: making long lists of favorite flowers, planning where spring bulbs will come up, calculating the percentage of perennials versus annuals. But as anyone who has ever tended a garden for more than four seasons will tell you, great ones aren't defined only by big, bountiful blooms. Memorable gardens show their true colors with the wind howling and the temperatures far south of picnic weather—when the so-called bones are most visible.

A garden's bones comprise the underlying architecture of any outdoor planting space. They provide the structure that makes a place feel grounded and the framework for everything else, in a sense the skeleton of the garden. They are what you see when the high-season color and bounty of all the flowers and deciduous trees and shrubs have vanished—usually during winter.

Hedges, fences, arbors, pergolas, paths, pools, topiaries, outbuildings, trees, statuary, terraces—the permanent features—all work together to form these bones, giving a garden shape and interest. They help establish the garden's personality.

> A garden's bones comprise the underlying architecture of any outdoor planting space.

Gardeners creating a new garden, then, would be well advised to put some serious time and thought into planning this foundational base before planting. At the height of the growing season, when herbaceous plants fill the beds, the bones are not apparent. But a garden's appeal should not be limited to spring and summer. The true test of a well-designed yard is the interest it offers when the only things visible are the hardscape along with the hedges and arbors and evergreens. If these have been placed with careful intent, the garden remains appealing despite its lack of color. It will have what the garden designer John Brookes called "winter drama."

Border

Borders, the glory of gardens, are ornamental, linear, and bursting with flowers and foliage. Usually they are backed by a fence, wall, or hedge. A border is longer than it is wide; a sweeping (and ambitious) border might be twelve feet deep and 100 or more feet long. A more modest border could be as small as three by five feet. At minimum, a border needs to be wide enough to hold at least three and preferably more layers of plants, but not so wide you cannot work in it. Often a two-foot-wide space is left between the border and the backing, for access, or a few stepping stones can be placed within the garden to facilitate weeding.

Borders in formal gardens are long rectangles with straight, crisp edges. The double border, popularized during the Edwardian era, consists of two parallel borders with a path in between. Double borders might be identical or different but harmonious—if one side receives more shade than the other, for instance. Of course, if the enclosed landscape is round, such as a circular lawn, the border echoes that. The edges of borders can be softened by allowing some plants to spill out.

Borders originated less than 200 years ago, but have their roots deeper in history. Monks in the Middle Ages planted around the periphery of their gardens. Seventeenth-century parterres and herb gardens were often edged with narrow borders. Victorian and Edwardian families that had neither the time nor money for fancy bedding schemes kept casual borders of familiar perennials and flowers gathered from the hedgerows, or grown from neighbors' clippings.

By the early nineteenth century, botanist, landscape gardener, and writer John Claudius Loudon was writing about garden borders and offering his advice on how best to create them. He devoted considerable space to them in his *Encyclopaedia of Gardening*, first published in 1822. As a response to landscape gardening, and influenced by Italian gardens, he advocated for what he called the "gardenesque" style of landscape design. He discussed common "mingled"

> At minimum, a border needs to be wide enough to hold at least three and preferably more layers of plants, but not so wide you cannot work in it.

flower borders, explaining that the goal was to have something in bloom through-out the season. To achieve this, many species were included, lined up in straight rows, with the tallest in the back and the shortest in front. There was a ring of space around each plant. His idea of mingled meant combining many different flowers in one border—but did *not* extend to letting the flowers touch each other!

Herbaceous borders, planted entirely with hardy perennials, are often extolled as the epitome of the English garden style. However, today most borders include bulbs and annuals as well, and often grasses. The designs of Piet Oudolf of the Netherlands and his followers are the exception. Oudolf revolutionized border design in the 1980s as part of the New Perennial Movement. His massed plant-ings are evocative of prairies and meadows. He fills his borders with blocks and swaths of perennials that he chooses for structure and durability. His choices, their seedpods, stalks, and the seed heads of grasses, look good in winter and are not cut down until almost spring. He favors grasses, sedums, asters, salvias, and other rugged perennials planted in masses. There are flowers in his borders, but they are not the main attraction. Oudolf's designs for the acclaimed High Line in New York City and Lurie Garden at Millennium Park in Chicago reflect these practices.

Mixed borders include shrubs in addition to perennials, bulbs, annuals, and often grasses. They offer the gardener many possibilities. It is easier to achieve a longer season with a mixed border than with an herbaceous border. Mixed borders, with their inclusion of shrubs, also add winter interest, especially if the shrubs have interesting bark or are evergreen. One scheme for a mixed border is 5 percent shrubs (not counting those in a backing hedge), 75 percent perennials, 10 percent bulbs and 10 percent annuals. An increased percentage of shrubs in the mixed border lowers the maintenance requirements. You can also add vines, to grow up a wall if you have one, or, if you are careful not to plant anything too aggressive, to intermingle with the perennials.

A border can also be made entirely of annuals, or annuals and half-hardy perennials. A blend of cosmos, cleome, nicotiana, and perhaps dahlia will offer months of bloom.

Typically, border plantings ascend in height from front to back. This allows visibility of all plants and nothing is blocked. Visual momentum can be added, however, if heights are mixed within the border. Tall plants can be placed in front of shorter ones if they are airy enough to see through. Or you can plant so your border undulates from one end to the other, intermittently varying heights. The slope from front to back can be varied.

Texture and plant shape are also a consideration: spiky, billowy; fuzzy leaves, leathery leaves; flat flower heads, mop-headed blooms. You want harmony and variety.

Borders in informal gardens are often curved. This can be a long sweep, a French curve, or a slight undulation.

Gardeners disagree on whether to cut borders down in fall or spring. There are compelling arguments on both sides. If you cut a border down in fall, it looks tidy for winter and saves time in spring. Fall cleanup also helps prevent some diseases and insect infestations. If not cut down, as with Oudolf's borders, remaining stems can offer some winter protection for plants and insurance against heaving. Seed heads provide food for wildlife and a foil for the bleakness of winter. You can also compromise and leave those plants with interesting pods and seed heads— such as baptisia and monarda—and chop down the rest.

The Border Ladies

It was the British garden designer and author Gertrude Jekyll, admiring the informal gardens around the old cottages of her Surrey home (and influenced by her friend William Robinson's tirades against the practice of bedding out), who popularized planting color-coordinated drifts of herbaceous perennials in borders. She collected plants from nearby fields, woodlands, and from the old-time gardens she admired. A painter and craftswoman, she believed that color played a key role in a border, and paid close attention to the way colors interacted with each other. She wanted hues to flow from one to another.

Jekyll also believed that "a flower border is seen to the best advantage when it has some solid backing such as a wall or an evergreen hedge." Though she favored the way the dark green of hollies and yews set off flowers, she was known to personally build stone walls to back her own borders. Today, borders might also be backed by a picket, stockade, or split-rail fence; the side of a shed; a greenhouse; or a latticed trellis.

Jekyll influenced many succeeding garden designers, including Beatrix Farrand, Vita Sackville-West, and Marian Coffin. Her influence continues today.

In 1908, Helena Rutherfurd Ely published *A Woman's Hardy Garden* at the urging of friends who sought her horticultural advice. Though she admired English borders, she assured her readers that they were not at fault if their own gardens did not look like those in England. She pointed out that the American climate is harsher, with summers hotter and winters colder than in England. Plants that could be grown in England perished in her own New Jersey garden. English gardening books, she said, were "useless" to the American gardener.

Like Jekyll, Ely had an aversion to the bedding style. She told her readers that beds of "Coleus, Geraniums, Verbenas . . . have passed away." Ely forbade her readers to make beds scattered about the lawn. She wanted her house first clothed in vines. After the vines were planted, she told her readers, start with one border at a time: a border on each side of the house, one across the front, near the street, followed by borders backed with shrubs along the boundaries with neighbors. She dug Virginia creeper from the woods several miles away and transplanted it at her house. She planted seeds, divided established plants, swapped with neighbors and tradesmen, and suggested that her readers could do the same.

Ely did not want to see bare earth in her borders as Loudon preferred, but she did want her plants in rows, broken up by occasional "clumps." She suggested a row of hollyhocks "three deep, broken every ten feet or so by a clump of a dozen," then a row of rudbeckias, phloxes, and so on.

Fifteen years later, Louise Beebe Wilder published *Colour in My Garden*. She corresponded with both Jekyll and Robinson, but, like Ely, felt the English garden style was not climatically possible in the United States. She believed that planting a border with drifts by color looked artificial and was too labor intensive, but like Jekyll she wanted formal structure with informal planting. Her answer for American borders was to create "pictures" within the border. The same spot might have three different pictures in a season. When an area was not a picture, because the plants were not flowering, foliage would keep it looking fresh. She too wanted no bare earth. Perhaps most interestingly, she thought gardeners who based their color scheme on the colors that were prevalent each season could not fail: yellow and white for early spring, rose color for late spring, blue and yellow for midsummer, and scarlet, gold, and purple for the end of the season.

Vita Sackville-West famously created a white garden at Sissinghurst to peak in July and August of 1951 for the Festival of Britain. Her monochromatic border became a status symbol emulated by gardeners around the world. Lawrence Johnston had laid out his daring red borders in his Hidcote gardens in Gloucestershire, England, by 1910. They were later nurtured and tweaked by nurseryman and author Graham Stuart Thomas. Thomas believed the secret to making a red garden was that "red containing yellow should not be mixed with red containing blue." Ely thought monochromatic gardens were merely a challenging exercise, not a feat to be copied.

Borrowed View, View, Vista

A borrowed view is an attractive feature in the landscape outside the garden perimeter, such as a mountain, pasture, or church spire, that is incorporated into the experience of the garden. With a borrowed view, you see just enough to have a sense of the feature, to add intrigue, yet the garden itself remains the main experience. Borrowing a view beyond the boundaries can make even a small garden feel expansive and add to its overall interest.

Though perhaps breathtakingly beautiful, a view outside the garden that has not been deliberately framed and made a controlled feature can overwhelm the garden. Our eyes are naturally drawn to the spectacle on the horizon. The flowers, shrubs, paths, arbors, and benches are secondary to the view.

Chinese gardeners were masters of the borrowed view. Philosophers such as Shao Yung extolled the happiness that a borrowed view brought him in his tiny garden in the eleventh century. Chinese gardens borrowed the sight of distant temples, mountains, a neighbor's flowers, even the sky, framing them with the curved eves of the house, a moon gate, or an opening in a bamboo grove.

Philosophers such as Shao Yung extolled the happiness that a borrowed view brought him in his tiny garden.

Japanese gardeners also took advantage of *shakkei*, or borrowed scenery, particularly from the sixth to the sixteenth centuries. They used borrowed views to create pictures, balancing the garden with the world beyond.

Today, we might borrow a neighbor's flowering tree, a pretty old barn, or a cityscape. The gardener must be a keen observer of what lies without—what might be highlighted as well as what must be blocked, such as an ugly cell tower.

A view can also be a scene within a garden, such as a glimpse of a parterre from a balcony, or of a pool, statue, or building from elsewhere in the garden. Here, the gardener creates the view itself, and, through judicious planting, directs visitors' attention to it. The great landscape gardeners of the eighteenth century were masters of this. They placed temples on islands that could be seen from the shore, built hermit huts to be spied from a distance, and carefully chose where trees should be planted—and removed—to provide the best viewing.

Vista is often used interchangeably with view, though it always connotes a pleasing view. Some landscape historians limit the meaning to a long view, or a narrow view that is framed. It might be the prospect at the end of an avenue lined with trees as well as the avenue and the trees themselves.

Botanical Garden, Collector's Garden

A botanical garden is a public garden established for scientific study, collection, cultivation, and preservation; plants in such gardens are labeled and displayed. (Many older public gardens use "botanic" in their official names. This term was favored in earlier eras; "botanic" and "botanical" are both correct.) Early botanical gardens, established in the sixteenth and seventeenth centuries, were physic gardens focused on the study of plants for medicinal purposes. A botanical garden for this purpose was established at the University of Pisa in 1543 and the University of Oxford Botanic Garden was founded in 1621.

The seventeenth and eighteenth centuries saw plant hunters traverse the globe in search of specimens and seeds, thus changing the direction of botanical gardens from the physic style to vast collections of plants from distant lands. Kew and other botanical gardens built glass conservatories for the exotic plants in their collections. John Bartram, the American botanist, explorer, and horticulturalist, kept a personal botanical garden behind his house in Philadelphia.

The United States Botanic Garden was founded in 1850 and has been in continuous operation since. Today, there are well over a thousand botanical gardens. Many focus on conservation and preservation as well as scientific study and public education.

Private collectors' gardens tend to focus on one or more specific plants, though there are collectors who seek as many different plants as possible.

Bridge

The first bridges were opportunistic—boulders that crossed a stream or the trunks of fallen trees that reached from one shore to the opposite—and allowed our earliest ancestors to get from one bank of a river or stream to the other without getting their feet wet. In time, ancient peoples were building bridges for themselves, using logs and later beams and boards.

The ancient Romans, who discovered and mastered both the arch and concrete, built arched masonry bridges on concrete piles throughout their empire. With this technology, they could span far greater distances than possible with flat beam bridges. Their bridges were strong enough to support large armies, chariots, and horses.

Medieval bridges such as the Old London Bridge, which relied on Roman methods, were lined with busy shops and sometimes houses. The Incas developed the suspension bridge, using ropes—a technology that so impressed the Spaniards, they introduced it to Europe. The first major iron bridge was made in Shropshire, England, in 1781, followed by steel bridges. Throughout history, bridges played a vital role in commerce, facilitating the entry of goods into towns and cities and shortening trade routes.

But it was gardeners who saw bridges as not just an efficient means to cross water, but as an element of pleasure and beauty. Moon bridges with tall, rounded arches were built over Chinese canals so that pedestrians could cross while boats passed beneath. When reflected, the image in the water together with the bridge itself formed a circle, or moon. Moon bridges, and later flattened versions, became a major design feature in Chinese and subsequent Japanese gardens. They were made of stone or wood, the wood often painted bright red. These bridges were admired by artists as well as gardeners and their guests, and appeared in paintings, woodblock prints, and ink wash drawings. They were meant to be viewed.

Some Chinese bridges had roofs or included pavilions. *The Mustard Seed Garden Manual of Painting*, the famous book of paintings named for the writer

> Medieval bridges such as the Old London Bridge . . . were lined with busy shops and sometimes houses.

Li Yu's tiny seventeenth-century Mustard Seed Garden of Nanking tells us that bridges were to be "savored" and that they were a place where "one could linger." Visitors could sip tea or wine, write poetry, and enjoy the surrounding landscape from the deck of a bridge, or gaze down at the mirror-like lake below.

Japanese gardens, which were imbued with philosophical meaning, featured flat bridges as well as moon bridges. If water was not available, it was suggested by sand and rocks. Bridges were also made by placing mossy stepping stones across a stream.

Bridges played an important visual role in the English landscape movement. Capability Brown built or incorporated bridges in many of his gardens, including the Vanbrugh Bridge at Blenheim, and the Palladian bridge at Stowe. His bridges, built of stone, sometimes with balustrades—and in the case of the Palladian, with a temple-like covering—were framed by hills, meadows, and distant forests. They served as focal points in the pictures he was forming in the landscape and are often photographed today.

The impressionist artist Claude Monet hired a craftsman to build a Japanese-style arched bridge over his pond. An avid horticulturalist, Monet created his gardens as a place to stroll and entertain as well as a place to paint. He painted his garden bridge numerous times, producing some of his most famous and beloved works and inspiring arched bridges in gardens throughout the world.

Bridge construction requires skilled engineering. Potential flooding, weather, and soil conditions must be taken into account. Pilings must be suitable for the underlying ground. Costs can be high. Nevertheless, a bridge adds to the garden experience. It can be made of masonry, metal, or wood. Wood is the least expensive but requires the most maintenance.

Small, ready-made bridges are widely available. They work well over a narrow or seasonal stream and can be used where the illusion of a stream is created with rocks. They can also be a charming addition to artificial ponds and streams, though careful thought must be given to size so a bridge doesn't overwhelm the water feature it's spanning.

A modern twist on the garden bridge is the bridge as garden. The Bridge of Flowers in Shelburne Falls, Massachusetts, is an old trolley bridge that has been retrofitted as a garden and is now a thriving tourist attraction. Other towns with bridges that no longer serve their original purpose, especially old manufacturing communities, are turning their bridges into public gardens.

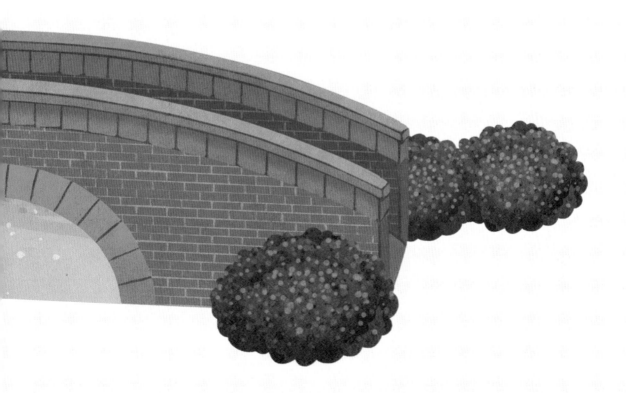

Cloche

A cloche is a bell-shaped glass vessel that is used to shelter tender plants and seedlings. The glass blower who invented the device has been lost to history, but we know that by the early seventeenth century they were being used in French gardens (*cloche* is French for "bell"), quickly spreading to English gardens and beyond. By the 1660s, John Evelyn, writing in *Elysium Britannicum, or The Royal Gardens*, thought cloches crucial enough to include in his illustrated list of necessary "instruments belonging to a gardener," calling them "Bells of Glasse . . . to shade plants, preserve them from haile, etc."

Glass was expensive at the time, so ordinary gardeners could not afford to protect their prized seedlings with cloches. However, the wealthy massed them in rows in the vegetable and melon beds of their walled gardens. With a cloche, the soil could be warmed and seeds could be started early. Mini-greenhouses invented at a time when greenhouses did not exist, cloches magnified the warmth from the sun, kept out wind and hail, and protected against frost.

Early cloches, usually a foot across, could vary slightly in shape, with some more flared at the base than others. Most had knobs at the top so that they could be lifted easily.

The thick glass was clear or light green; many gardeners preferred the green tint. John Claudius Loudon writes in his *Encyclopaedia of Gardening* that common glass bells were made of "bottle-glass" and were "used in the open garden for protecting cauliflower or other culinary plants, or for striking cuttings, or for retaining a moist atmosphere about seeds." He goes on to discuss lighter bells, what he calls a "crystal bell, or receiver," which he tells us is "generally three to eight inches in diameter, and from four inches to one foot in height. These glasses are employed in striking tender cuttings in the exotic departments."

Hand lights were in use at the same time. These cloches were constructed of lead, copper, or iron frames with multiple small panes of glass in various shapes including hexagons, triangles, and rectangles. Some bell-shaped cloches were also made with metal frames rather than blown.

By the Victorian era, both types of cloches had proliferated, with hand lights dominating. As the season progressed, the cloches and lights would be removed and stacked out of the way, until they were needed at the end of the season to safeguard plants from the oncoming cold.

With a cloche, the soil could be warmed and seeds could be started early.

Cloches were also made, less expensively, of terra-cotta. These bottomless, often two-foot-tall jars had lids that could be removed for ventilation. Such cloches had a different purpose altogether: to force rhubarb and to blanch (stop photosynthesis and retain tenderness) celery and asparagus. Gardeners referred to them as "forcers," "blanchers," and "shades" as well as cloches. Thomas Jefferson used both glass and terra-cotta cloches at Monticello, including blanchers for sea kale.

In the twentieth century, continuous cloches came into widespread use. There were tent cloches, which were made of two pieces of glass placed at right angles like a tent; barn cloches which were similar to the tents, but with vertical glass sides; and barn cloches with flat glass tops.

Today, plastic has supplanted glass and terra-cotta. We have plastic cloches (you can make one yourself by cutting the bottom from a plastic milk carton), row covers, tunnels, and walls of water (plastic structures filled with water to hold the heat longer). There are also bamboo and chicken wire cloches. These act more as cages than greenhouses. They are meant to keep critters—rabbits, chipmunks, deer—from nibbling treasured plants. In reality, you will want something sturdier if your goal is to protect your plants from feasting wildlife, but wire and bamboo cloches are decorative and add a touch of yesterday to the garden.

The same can be said for classic glass and terra-cotta cloches. Antique specimens are much sought after. Reproductions are offered in garden shops and online catalogs. Today they are placed in the garden more for their beauty and as a reminder of a bygone era than for practicality. Cloches have morphed from Evelyn's necessary tool to today's ornament, but there is no reason they cannot also be used. They not only look good, they work.

Cold Frame

Cold frames are bottomless boxes with slanted glass or clear plastic tops which are used to extend the growing season. In the spring, they can be used to harden off seedlings or to start plants. In the autumn, they can be used to grow salad greens or give a few weeks of protection to tender plants. Typically, the frame is longer than it is wide, with the back higher than the front. The footprint can vary, depending upon available space, materials, and needs. The glass or plastic top is hinged, so it can be easily lifted for access and ventilation.

A cold frame can be placed directly on garden soil, over a pit, or on blocks, pavers, or bricks. A pit provides the added insulation of the earth, but it can flood during heavy rains. Alternatively, a pit can be filled with manure that has not yet rotted; the heat from the manure turns the pit into a hot bed. Hot beds have been made since antiquity and are popular with organic growers.

Seeds or seedlings can be directly planted, or pots can be used in the cold frame. Care must be taken that the box does not overheat from solar gain during the day. The top should be opened for ventilation on all the but the coldest, cloudiest days, and closed at night. Plants inside will need to be watered. On very cold nights, the cold frame can be covered with blankets for added protection, or the box can be surrounded with hay bales. Heating coils can be added to aid in germination, but a cold frame is not a heated greenhouse. It is not intended for winter gardening in frigid climates.

Cold frames are best placed in a sunny but protected spot, facing south in the Northern Hemisphere. Many gardeners place them near the back door or near the greenhouse for easy access. Though they can be removed during summer, they are often so attractive that they are left in place.

Drawings of seventeenth-century cold frames look identical to those typically used today; the basic design has remained unchanged. At first, frames had multiple small panes of glass, but soon the Dutch cold frame was introduced with a single pane. This let in more light but was more expensive to repair if the glass broke.

With simple carpentry skills, you can easily build a cold frame with scrap or repurposed wood (pressure-treated wood should not be used). Old windows

work well for the glass top and add charm, though caution should be taken to ensure that any window paint does not contain lead. Of course, a functional and pretty cold frame can be made with all new materials. The box can be made of bricks or cement blocks for a permanent cold frame. A temporary frame can be made with straw bales arranged to form a box and covered with glass. Aluminum and polycarbonate cold frames are commercially available, as are frames built of cedar. Many can be quickly disassembled for easy storage or transport to another part of the garden.

Community Garden

A community garden is a public or private plot of land that has been set aside or rescued so that local residents, particularly those without land of their own, can have a place to grow fresh, healthy fruits and vegetables and flowers for pleasure. Some community gardens are completely shared. In others, individuals tend their own gardens within the larger space.

In addition to being a place to grow food and flowers, community gardens provide participants with a place to enjoy the outdoors, camaraderie, and physical exercise. Some gardens are formed by a particular group of people so they can grow the foods of their country of origin, often not available in grocery stores. Others are formed to reclaim a vacant city lot that has become an eyesore. Some community gardens primarily grow food for a local soup kitchen or school.

Community gardens are located in city neighborhoods, at residential complexes, in hospitals, and in schoolyards. Besides necessary permits or consent, the only requirements are ample sun, access to water, and interested gardeners.

Besides necessary permits or consent, the only requirements are ample sun, access to water, and interested gardeners.

Community gardens are generally volunteer driven but have a governing structure. They can be set up informally, formally as a nonprofit, or as an entity of the property owner, such as with a senior housing center. Many parks and recreation departments or other municipal entities support community gardens, though this can lead to challenges when there are budgetary cutbacks. There are usually shared tasks, such as path maintenance, and common resources such as a water source, or heavy equipment. Some community gardens require a fee to cover expenses; others have a benefactor.

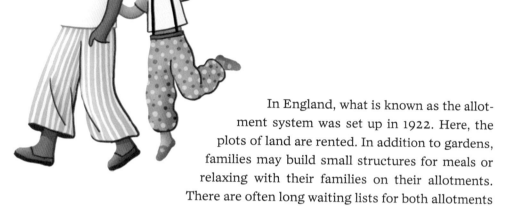

In England, what is known as the allotment system was set up in 1922. Here, the plots of land are rented. In addition to gardens, families may build small structures for meals or relaxing with their families on their allotments. There are often long waiting lists for both allotments and community gardens.

Predating community gardens and allotments was the practice of keeping agricultural fields and houses apart. In seventeenth- and eighteenth-century New England, colonists clustered their houses together for safety. The houses were often ringed around a shared green for grazing. The woman of the house might grow herbs, vegetables, and a few flowers close to the house, but the fields of corn, grain, and other crops would be grown away from the houses, or in long, narrow back lots. English villagers of the same time period and earlier had fields outside the town proper.

The American Community Garden Association formed in 1982 as a nonprofit to support the community garden movements in the United States and Canada, and to serve as a hub for resources. Since then, the movement has grown, as more people see the value of communal cultivation.

Compost Bin

The first written account of people mixing decaying organic matter for fertilizer appears on clay tablets from King Sargon's reign, during the Akkadian Empire in present day Iraq, around 2300 BCE. It describes manure compost. There is also evidence of early composting in China (cooked bones, manure, and silkworm debris), India, and some experts contend, in situ composting as much as 12,000 years ago in Scotland. Ancient peoples likely noticed that the plants that sprang up where there was rotting plant matter and livestock waste were particularly robust.

Cleopatra was so taken with the work that worms do in making compost that she protected them, decreeing that any Egyptian who took worms out of the country would be put to death. In his old age, the Roman farmer and author Marcus Porcius Cato, Cato the Elder, wrote a reflective treatise on farming, in which he shared his agricultural advice. He counseled his fellow agrarians to make a big compost heap (or "manure") of "litter, lupine straw, chaff, bean stalks, husks, and the leaves of ilex and of oak."

William Shakespeare, Sir Francis Bacon, Sir Walter Raleigh, and other Renaissance writers mentioned compost in their works. Hamlet warns against adding compost to weeds "to make them ranker."

George Washington, determined to discover how best to improve his soil, tested composts made of different ingredients. He had a stercorary, or dung repository, built near his stables at Mount Vernon, a precursor to and rather glorified version of our compost bins. Beneath was a pit, lined with cobblestones. Above was an open-sided, post-and-beam structure with a peaked roof. Near the ridge line, he added perches for birds, so their droppings would be efficiently captured for the compost. Washington combined quantities of stable manure with waste plant material from the farm to make his compost. A reconstruction of his stercorary is on exhibit at Mount Vernon today.

The art of composting was largely forgotten during the West's love affair with chemical fertilizers and pesticides. This changed when Jerome Rodale, founder of Rodale Press, read *An Agricultural Treatment*, by Sir Albert Howard. Howard had spent almost fifty years in India where he made it his mission to increase the fertility of the depleted soil. He faced obstacles. Dung was burned for fuel and so was not an option. Chemical fertilizers were too costly. Having read about Chinese composting, he ultimately developed what he called the Indore composter, after the town where he worked. Howard layered vegetable waste with manure and turned his concoction on a regular schedule. During much of the year, this was done in pits, but during the monsoon season, he composted above ground. Deeply impressed, Rodale became an ardent evangelist for organic farming and composting and began his own sixty-acre organic farm in Pennsylvania. To promote his ideas, he started a magazine, *Organic Farming and Gardening* with the tagline, "Back to Nature in Agriculture," and sent 12,000 complimentary copies of the first edition in May 1942 to American farmers.

Compost heaps are still used, but a bin, or series of bins provides more control and tidiness. An inexpensive and surprisingly attractive bin can be made from recycled wood pallets. Three pallets stood on end and wired together to form a U shape make a durable and functional bin. This can easily be extended into a double or triple bin so that compost in various stages of readiness can be maintained. From the back, it looks like fence. A more finished-looking yet simple four-sided bin can made with two-by-fours and wood slats. Instead of leaving the front open, the front side is removable.

Bins can also be built from cement blocks. Left unmortared, these can be dismantled and moved elsewhere should you redesign or expand the garden. A more organic bin can be constructed of straw bales, which eventually become compost themselves.

A simple bin, round or square, can be made of chicken wire affixed to stakes or a frame. The stakes can be pounded into the ground, and the wire stapled to them. Or, after the frame is built, wire can be attached. Large chicken wire bins are often preferred by gardeners with many autumn leaves to rake.

Most gardeners hide or camouflage their compost bins, tucking them in a far corner of the garden where they aren't obvious. But compost bins are an important working element of a garden, and can be attractive.

George Washington, determined to discover how best to improve his soil, tested composts made of different ingredients.

Nevertheless, if you do not wish them to be visible, they can be screened with hedges, a trellis, or fencing. Attractive or not, most gardeners will set the bin up in a utility area rather than an ornamental part of the garden.

Interest in sustainability has led to considerable research into composting and the development of tumblers, and other improved compost bins. These modern bins are made of green or black plastic, resin, or metal, often raised up on legs, some with drawers. They are enclosed to keep hungry and curious animals out. Some accommodate worms. Most produce compost more quickly than old-fashioned or homemade bins.

Cottage Garden

Cottage gardens originated in the early Middle Ages of England. Peasants, families of husbandmen, laborers, small leaseholders, and artisans such as potters and blacksmiths enclosed their plots (often an eighth or quarter of an acre) with hedgerows, so they could provide for their needs and keep their animals from roaming. The privy would be in back and maybe a shed. There would be a few fruit trees, some berries, herbs, vegetables, and greens all planted close together. Tucked in here and there would be flowers. There would be livestock, such as chickens, a pig, maybe a cow. Access paths wound throughout the tiny lot. Every square inch of ground was used.

These were make-do-with-what-you-have gardens. Growers enriched their soil with horse droppings swept from the lane as well as manure from their own livestock They divided their plants, collected seeds, transplanted wildflowers from the roadside, and traded with their neighbors. They brought their prized plants inside for the winter.

By the seventeenth century, gardening for pleasure as well as subsistence became possible due to an improved British economy. Plants from distant lands began to arrive. Cottage gardens became more floriferous, multicolored with a "bit of this, and a bit of that." Daniel Defoe exclaimed over them in his book, *Tour Through the Whole Island of Great Britain*, saying that you could not stand on high ground above any village without being taken with the houses "surrounded with gardens." The influential British garden writer and magazine publisher John Claudius Loudon wrote at the beginning of the nineteenth century that "almost every cottage in England has its appendant garden."

If the cottage was close to the road, the entire front might be given over to flowers, with food crops and livestock relegated to the back. Cottagers whose houses were set back from the road would line the front walk with violets, primroses, and other flowers, and keep the food crops off to the side. Vegetables might be planted in rows to facilitate hoeing and harvesting, but the flowers were tucked in here and there and jumbled together. Some villages held horticultural competitions in which flowers were judged and packets of seeds were generally awarded as prizes. Cottage gardeners who grew their flowers for competition were known as florists.

During the eighteenth century, with the rise of the landscape movement, many wealthy landowners cleared the rustic workers' cottages from their estates, so that these humble abodes and their blowsy gardens would not mar the pastoral views the gentry were trying to achieve. Though some land owners built new villages for the people they had displaced, many did not.

Cottage gardens were further threatened as the Industrial Revolution wrought cultural change and upheaval. It was no longer necessary for a household to produce all its own food. Trains moved butter, cheese, and other foodstuffs great distances at remarkable speeds. Large-scale centralized production became the norm. Factories lured young people to the city in search of work. Factory smoke hung in the air, stressing shrubs and trees. The fad for carpet bedding featuring blocks of brightly colored annuals from Africa and South America transformed fashionable gardens.

Then, at the end of the eighteenth century and well into the nineteenth, with the scourge of air pollution, came the idea that fresh air was curative. Artists, writers, and intellectuals extolled the virtues of country life. The Arts and Crafts Movement took hold and with it, a wave of nostalgia for cottage gardens. This nostalgia was furthered by a few writer-gardeners and artists who had themselves come under the spell of the pretty cottage garden. Preeminent garden writers such as William Robinson and Gertrude Jekyll championed the aesthetics of cottage gardens. The artist Helen Allingham romanticized them. Beatrix Potter filled children's minds and hearts with indelible images of cottage gardens with her book, *The Tale of Peter Rabbit*.

Today, the cottage garden is a style. It is reflective of a past, real and imagined, updated for the twenty-first century. A cottage garden can be tiny, as many were in the past, or up to an acre or so, but it is, by definition, always close to the house. Cottage gardens are intimate. There are no grand vistas or allées. There are jumbles and tangles of flowers and vines sprawling over the walks, draped over arbors, climbing the walls, all seemingly casually placed. Fences and gates are made of wood. This is not the place for fancy wrought iron or shiny vinyl. There might be a birdbath or a small pond, but large statues and stone urns are best left to other gardens. Bee skeps, watering cans, and clay flowerpots are at home. Paths are beaten earth, gravel, local stone, or rosey brick. Outbuildings such as a repurposed privy, shed, or small barn fit nicely. Stone walls and troughs add interest. A bench in the sun where you can sit and shell peas or gossip with a friend is a fitting addition.

It is not necessary to be a purist about plants. Heirlooms are welcome, but there are many modern cultivars that have the same look and feel as old cottage favorites. Happily, they are less prone to disease and pests. Perennials, biennials, annuals, bulbs, vines, vegetables, herbs, and fruits can all have a role in the cottage garden.

A cottage garden feels relaxed and inviting. However, it is more labor intensive than many other types of gardens. It requires diligent and knowledgeable tending. A mature cottage garden is just shy of descending into a jungle-like mess of rampant overgrowth and requires a firm hand to keep it on the right side of chaos.

Creating a modern cottage garden is more about embracing the spirit of those early gardens than attempting a historical restoration. Cottagers were improvisers. They relied on local materials. They made things and they loved plants. The same can be said of modern cottage gardeners.

Cutting Garden

A cutting garden is devoted to flowers that will be cut and brought indoors for display in vases or to dry for later use. The flowers can be grown as a crop in rows, or in raised beds with paths. They might be part of a cottage garden, take up a corner of the vegetable garden or have a space all their own, depending upon how many flowers are desired. The garden should be sited in full sun, with good soil, and out of view, away from the main gardens. Because the garden is devoted to flowers that will be cut, gaps and the overall appearance are not a primary concern.

Flowers can include annuals, such as cosmos, sunflowers, celosia, zinnias, and snapdragons, or bulbs such as daffodils and gladioli. Perennials might include peonies, globe thistle, chrysanthemums, delphiniums, iris, lilies, or Russian sage. Roses, too, have been important in the cutting garden. Generally, flowers with long stems are best. One also needs to consider blooming times and what flowers will work well together in a vase.

Han Dynasty Chinese favored the peony above all flowers to fill their beautiful vases. Ancient Egyptians also filled their vases with cut flowers, including iris and scilla. In the seventh century, the Japanese developed a ritualistic form of flower arranging called ikebana, to decorate their altars and later their homes. British and European churches required an abundance of cut flowers for their services, which their parishioners supplied.

Despite the constant harvesting of flowers, a cutting garden can be beautiful. Celia Thaxter famously cut armfuls of flowers from her garden early every morning to fill the vases in her summer cottage and for the hotel she ran with her family. In her book, *An Island Garden*, she describes the "massed nasturtiums," marigolds, coreopsis, dahlias, Shirley poppies, tea roses, and Madonna lilies that she had arranged at various heights on the tops of low bookcases, on tables, and throughout the room where she received guests. The American impressionist artist Childe Hassam, who was often Thaxter's guest, not only painted lush watercolors of the flower-filled room, he painted the cutting garden itself, illustrating its extravagance of bloom. Today, Thaxter's garden has been restored and is open for limited visits.

Courtyard

A courtyard is an enclosed outdoor space. It can be bound by multiple buildings, such as a house and its outbuildings, or set within a single building. A courtyard provides light and air to the buildings it serves as well as privacy, a place to gather, and a sheltered spot for a garden.

Archaeologists have excavated courtyard houses in the Jordan River Valley from 6400–6000 BCE; in the city of Ur, in modern day Iraq, dating to 2000 BCE; and in various other sites throughout the Mediterranean region. Ancient Roman courtyards (atriums) featured pools, potted plants, fountains, statues, and al fresco dining. Traditional and historic mosques and residences in Islamic culture were centered on a courtyard or *sahn*. The residential courtyard, a private garden, would be used for family meals and entertaining. In China, traditional courtyard gardens are formed by a compound of family houses that share a central courtyard or, sometimes with the growth of the family and construction of more houses, multiple courtyards.

Small Japanese courtyard gardens, or *tsuboniwa*, depart from the concept of courtyard gardens as living spaces and are instead created for viewing. One can look out upon the courtyard

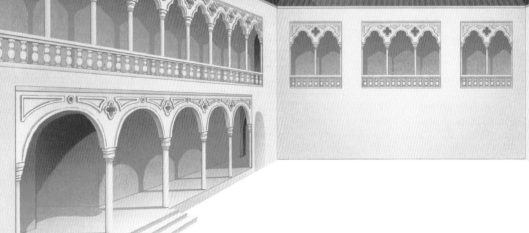

garden from within the house and gain a sense of nature and tranquility from the symbolism inherent in the stones, lantern, water, moss, and often bonsai that grace the tiny space.

Thomas Church, the influential landscape architect who pioneered modernist principles in gardening and wrote *Gardens Are for People*, chose a courtyard garden when making a garden for himself. Located in San Francisco, his intimate courtyard garden was on the side of his house. He furnished it with a gravel floor, a white table and chairs, a few artifacts he had collected, and a pair of elephant statues to hold plants. There was a lush rose hedge along one wall, a balustrade, and potted plants. Most interestingly, he made an unusual parterre in an abstract design, with curves as well as straight lines, giving the garden freshness and inviting conversation.

New York City boasts a number of famous courtyard gardens. The Dakota, a New York cooperative apartment building constructed at the end of the nineteenth century and home to Lauren Bacall, Judy Garland, John Lennon, and many other creative people, has a spacious formal courtyard. During the early years of the twentieth century, the New York real estate speculator William Waldorf Astor built high-rent apartment buildings including Graham Court, the Belnord, and Apthorp, that all featured courtyards. Accessible only to residents, the courtyards featured fountains, brick walkways, and lavish plantings.

Art museums feature some of the most stunning courtyard gardens and can be enjoyed by the public. The Frick Collection in New York, the Isabella Stewart Gardner Museum in Boston, and the Getty Villa in Los Angeles are just a few worth visiting.

Because courtyards are generally square or rectangular and enclosed, they work well with a formal layout. They need to be attractive when looked upon from the surrounding windows as well as from within. And as Thomas Church showed, the restrictions imposed by the enclosed nature of a courtyard garden can lead to rich horticultural design innovation.

A courtyard provides light and air to the buildings it serves as well as privacy, a place to gather, and a sheltered spot for a garden.

Deck

Viewing decks have long been an integral part of Japanese gardens. Small, simple platforms made of wood or bamboo, they offer a place to gaze at the moon, to meditate on the ripples in a pond, or to admire a mossy rock. They are quiet stopping points in the garden where one can pause, reflect, and contemplate.

American decks are outdoor rooms with moderate to large footprints. By the third quarter of the twentieth century they had become a widespread garden feature, even in home landscapes that could scarcely be considered gardens. As suburbs spread and family life moved from the social front porch to the more private backyard, decks became a dominant feature. They were championed by the California designer Thomas Church. The word "deck" derives from the deck of a ship, originally *dec* in the fifteenth century, but Church liked to call them floating porches. He placed them close to the house, attached, or at a distance unattached, encouraging people to better enjoy their gardens by using their decks as a place to relax, entertain, dine, or observe the surrounding lawn, trees, and flowerbeds. Decks offer year-round outdoor living in warm climates such as California, but even in cooler climates, they can be used during the warmer months of spring and fall as well as summer.

Decks are made of wood, vinyl, manufactured wood, or wood composites. They can be built over uneven terrain, making them suitable for sites not level enough for a patio or terrace. They can also be built over sensitive environments such as water, wetlands, and dunes, enabling the owner and guests to enjoy these features without causing harm or disturbance.

In the United States, decks thirty inches or more above ground require railings at least thirty-six inches high, with vertical balusters spaced no more than four inches apart, though individual municipalities may have more stringent requirements than these national codes. Railings prevent people from falling off the deck, but they also present design opportunities. Deck railings can be made of the same material as the deck, of metal, or of a combination of materials. Styles range from turned and painted balusters, which give a colonial feel, to more contemporary designs in sleek, gleaming metal. They are often topped with planters such as traditional window boxes, grow bags, or coir baskets.

Decks can be multileveled, sheltered with trellises, lattice, or a pergola clothed in vines, and furnished with built-in benches and planters. They can be built around trees, providing shade and a sense of theater. Steps between levels and down to the ground facilitate movement and make a nice spot for a few flowerpots.

Decks, especially those attached to the house, connect the house and the garden, and extend each into the other. They provide a wonderful stage for container plants and outdoor living.

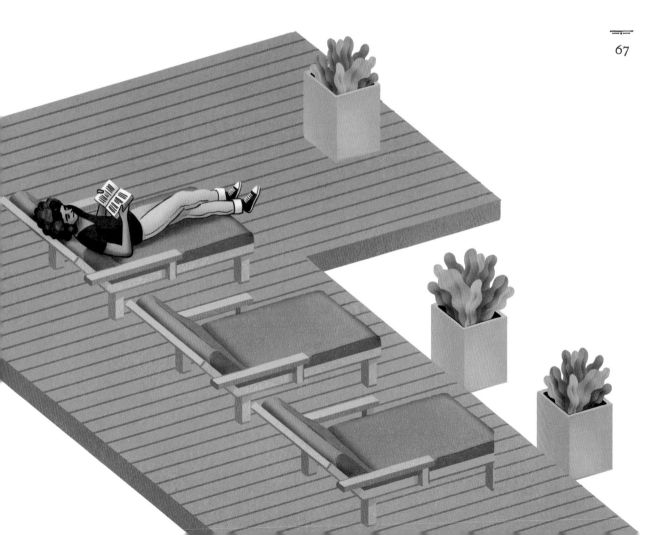

Edging

Edging delineates a space outlining the beds. It can be made of many different materials as well as living plants, giving the garden identity. A well-made edge sharpens the picture that the plants create.

The simplest and least expensive form of edging is a ditch or groove edge. It requires some work, diligence, and practice but is very effective. The gardener cuts a V-shaped groove a couple of times a season with a sharp, half-moon edging tool. All plant matter, especially roots, are removed from the groove while keeping the edge of the groove crisp and straight. It is something of a magic trick. A well-edged garden looks terrific even if the beds themselves are weedy. More than one gardener has rushed out and edged the borders when learning that visitors are on the way. With the edge freshly made, no one will notice that the bee balm needs deadheading or that a few thistles have popped up among the hollyhocks.

Gardeners have been improvising edging materials as long as there have been gardens, using everything from sheep bones to hub caps. Various hard materials, such as wood, metal, and ceramics, make more permanent edges and echo or set the tone of the garden. These can include palisades, fieldstones, cobblestones, bricks, tiles, timbers, willow and wattle, pavers, steel lawn strips, concrete, cast and wrought iron, rebar, wine bottles—even dinner plates.

> Gardeners have been improvising edging materials as long as there have been gardens, using everything from sheep bones to hub caps.

Willow and wattle, beautiful and ancient forms of edging, are essentially basketry. Used in herb gardens during the Middle Ages and later in European and North American gardens, they can be made from local materials or purchased ready-made. Willow is, needless to say, made from willow. Wattle is made from woods such as willow, ash, oak, or hazel. The wood must be used when newly cut and pliable. The edging can be woven solid or left with latticed openings. Some makers like to weave a fancy topping.

Cobblestones, first used by the Romans to pave their roads, occur naturally. Smoothed by water, the stones were gathered from rivers and streams. They were later used in fifteenth-century Europe and later still in North America. Setts, or Belgium bricks, are widely available today; they are quarried and cut granite stones sometimes mistakenly called cobblestones. Rectangular and consistent in size and shape, setts came into use in the nineteenth century. Antique cobblestones and setts are desirable and much sought after for edging. However, granite setts are still being made and quite indistinguishable from the antique stones.

Terra-cotta edging tiles were popular with the Victorians. The tiles, shaped somewhat like traditional gravestones, featured roped and half-roped tops, similar to some flowerpots of the era and earlier. There were "gothic" tiles, shaped into the traditional pointed arch. Some tiles were impressed on the front with geometric designs and flowers. Tiles were left unglazed or salt-glazed. They ranged in color from red to gray depending upon the clay used. The flames of the kiln gave individual tiles a lovely variation in hue; darker where the flames touched the clay. Some potteries continued to make edging tiles, along with other horticultural ware, into the twentieth century. Antique edging tiles can still be seen in gardens and cemeteries.

Online and antique shops specializing in garden ornaments offer old edging tiles for sale. A number of firms in the UK, Italy, Australia, and the United States, and some studio potters, make charming ceramic reproductions. There are also resin and cement versions available.

Boxwood edging has been the edging of choice for parterres, knot gardens, and herb gardens for centuries. Boxwood is easy to propagate, flourishes when clipped, remains green all year, and can be grown to whatever height you wish. Sadly, boxwood blight has struck gardens on both sides of the Atlantic, leaving unsightly, languishing, and too often dead plants in its wake.

But gardeners have successfully used other plants for living edging for centuries, so alternatives are to be had. Traditional alternatives include lavender, rosemary, and thyme.

Cast iron and wrought iron edgings are essentially very low decorative fences. Ornate, they sport such features as the fleur-de-lis, scrolls, and finials. Widespread in the nineteenth century, they graced urban and suburban formal gardens. Today antique versions, enhanced with the patina of years, are much sought after. Reproductions and new versions in lighter metals, including galvanized or powder-coated steel and aluminum, are readily available and easy to install.

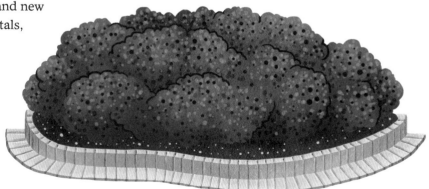

Espalier, Fan, Cordon

An attractive way to grow fruit trees, vines, or shrubs, create an interesting divider in the garden, or take advantage of the reflective warmth of a wall, is to create espaliers, fans, cordons, or double cordons.

Pruning and training plants into shapes they would not naturally achieve began with the grapevine, which is pliable. Egyptians trained their grapevines into arbors. The Romans, who spread a taste for wine as far north as Britain by 100 BCE, developed more elaborate shapes. However, it wasn't until the sixteenth century that the practice spread to fruit trees. Europeans began to prune and wire their trees against walls to protect them from the cold and produce more fruit. By the eighteenth century, gardeners appreciated the ornamental possibilities of such pruning.

For espalier, pairs of opposite branches or laterals are trained at a right angle to the vertical stem. The number of opposing arms is determined by how tall you want the espalier to be. Espaliers are usually grown against a wall but can be freestanding if posts and wires are used to train them. Other decorative effects are achieved by turning up the outstretched branches into a candelabra shape, or weaving them into a crisscrossed "Belgium fence," which looks a bit like lattice.

To form a cordon, only very short laterals are permitted on the vertical stem. Cordons are often trained at a 45-degree angle for space efficiency, but they can be grown upright. A double cordon is created by allowing two laterals to grow outward and slightly upward to form the bowl of a V or U shape, then forming each into a vertical. Like espaliers, cordons can be grown against a wall, or on wires to form an airy divider.

Similarly, fans are formed by pruning and training the plant into a fan shape. Other designs can be created as long as the training principles are followed.

Espalier brings formality to a garden. It makes it possible to grow a variety of fruits in a narrow space.

Fairy Garden

Gardeners have been infatuated with miniatures for thousands of years. In China, Daoists created miniature mystical landscapes as early as the first century. By the Tang Dynasty, the art of *penjing*, creating miniature landscapes in ceramic or bronze dishes, was in full flower. These sophisticated groupings featured tiny trees, mountains, and lakes. Japanese travelers brought some of the dish gardens home, where, influenced by Zen simplicity, the gardens evolved into a single heavily pruned and trained tree in a shallow ceramic dish: a style that would come to be known as bonsai.

Victorians used inherently diminutive alpine plants in their rock gardens to create miniature landscapes, sometimes scale models of actual landscapes. In the late nineteenth century, Lady Broughton created miniature mountains and valleys in imitation of the mountains of Savoy and the valley of Chamonix at her manor in Cheshire, England: Hoole House. Victorians also enjoyed creating miniature worlds in terrariums, which they enhanced with moss, pebbles, and sticks.

Meanwhile, fairies, elves, wood sprites, and wee folk occurred in pre-Industrial European folklore and superstition for centuries, perhaps millennia. They could be playful, mischievous, or threatening. Parents believed that fairies could steal a baby and take the infant's place, becoming a changeling—a fearful thought that explained children with birth defects or problematic behavior. Naturally occurring fairy rings and circles of mushrooms were evidence of reveling elves or dancing fairies. Unexpected mishaps and worse were blamed on fairies. In order to avoid their tricks and pranks, Europeans of the time believed it was provident to create a welcoming space for them with soft leaves for beds and other niceties.

A fairy garden might be as simple as a small, gothic-arched wooden door affixed to the base of a gnarled tree trunk.

In the 1950s, Anne Ashberry promoted miniature gardens as a solution for elderly, handicapped, and landless gardeners. Her book, *Miniature Gardens*, also intrigued gardeners who suffered from none of these inconveniences, and interest in miniature gardening spread first in the United States and then in the UK.

All of these historical threads are found in today's fairy gardens. A fairy garden might be as simple as a small, gothic-arched wooden door affixed to the base of a gnarled tree trunk. It might have a path of pea-sized flat stones leading up to the door, or perhaps a circle of ferns and violets. It can be made of little houses constructed of sheets of bark and moss, with acorn bowls and tables and chairs made of twigs, all tucked into a corner of a larger garden or nestled in a planter. Plants might include soft lamb's ears for beds, foxgloves for fairy bonnets, and hollyhocks for fairy skirts.

Garden centers and online specialty shops offer fairy houses, arbors, wells, picket fences, swings, bridges, and other accessories for creating a fairy garden, even little fairies themselves with gossamer wings. Yet everything in a fairy garden need not be miniature. In our collective imaginations, fairies are tiny but they inhabit our larger world. Miniature gardens, on the other hand, are entirely to scale, and not necessarily for fairies. They adhere to the same design principles and styles as full-size gardens. Like fairy gardens, they can be made indoors or out.

Fairy gardens can be enjoyed across generations, made together by parents, grandparents, and children. They are a way to introduce children to the world of gardening. Many house museums and public gardens feature them or host events around them. The Wee Faerie Village is an annual weeklong event at the Florence Griswold Museum in Old Lyme, Connecticut, with thirty artist-made, hand-crafted fairy homes displayed throughout the oft-painted gardens of Ms. Griswold. Numerous fairy garden events occur throughout the United States and UK, inspiring more gardeners to create their own in hidden, magical pockets of their larger landscapes.

Fence

A fence is a structure meant to mark a boundary, enclose a space, provide privacy, or act as a barrier. It can add definition to a garden, back a border, or serve as support for vines. Fences can be made of metal, wood, bamboo (treated like wood, but technically a grass), vinyl rails, or panels supported by posts. They can be both decorative and practical.

Gardeners first began walling their gardens to protect the property from thieves and intruders (both four-legged and two-legged). Later, their pleasing appearance also added to the popularity of fences.

Wattle fences, woven from willow or hazel withies (thin sticks), have been made since Neolithic times. European gardeners of the Middle Ages made wattle from withies which they cut from coppiced or pollarded trees. They used wattle to enclose their gardens, to make raised beds, and to enclose their sheep. Wattle fencing was made in place. Hurdles, which are also woven, were made in sections and movable. Today, a wattle fence adds rustic charm, especially to herb and vegetable gardens.

Stockade or palisade fences have been used for fortification since before the Romans. A simple palisade fence is shown enclosing a kitchen garden in Thomas Hill's *The Gardener's Labyrinth*, published in London in 1577. Today, stockade fences are mass produced in sections. Eight to twelve feet tall and opaque, they are primarily used as privacy screens. Less expensive than a brick or stone wall, they offer complete enclosure. Variations include tall, opaque fences made of solid, decorative panels, sometimes topped with openwork. Gardeners soften the look of stockade fences with large paintings, birdhouses, vertical planting, and of course vines.

By the mid-eighteenth century, European gardeners and homeowners embraced ornate wrought iron fencing. It was pretty and more durable than wood. Wrought iron did not widely appear in America until the end of the nineteenth century, when it graced the gardens of the wealthy urban gardens of the East Coast. Cast iron, which appeared around the same time, was equally ornate but mass-produced and affordable, bringing pretty metal fencing to the middle classes. Victorian gardeners loved the rich ornamental possibilities.

Though colonial Americans brought wattle-making skills with them, they soon turned to wood for fences, as it was abundant. They made stockade fences, board fences, picket fences, and split-rail fences.

Early split-rail fences were made of stacked rails, the ends of each section interlocked with the next. Sometimes called worm fences, they zigzagged across the land, taking up more ground than the fences the colonists had known in Europe. These fences were strong enough to keep livestock out of the garden, although, remarkably, they could be made by one person with few tools. Later, split-rail fences evolved into fences made of posts with holes to insert rails. Eventually, these fences contained livestock rather than protecting and marking gardens. In the 1950s, the post-and-rail style planted with red roses was favored as a street-front fence. Its popularity continues to this day.

White picket fences were seen as a mark of status from the beginning of the colonial era. Because their purpose was primarily decorative, they signified success. By the twentieth century, the white picket fence had become a symbol of the American dream: a house, marriage, and children. The simple beauty of these fences makes them an attractive addition to gardens today, whether they enclose a flower or vegetable garden within a larger property, or act as a street-front fence.

Board fences were used to keep livestock out of gardens. Now they are more often used to keep animals in their proscribed pastures, such as on horse farms. Still, they work well in informal gardens. Backed with chicken wire set deep in the earth, they are impenetrable to deer, woodchucks, rabbits, and such, yet retain the good looks of a board fence. The wire makes a nice support for vines.

Gardeners first began walling their gardens to protect the property from thieves and intruders (both four-legged and two-legged).

Industry has given us maintenance-free vinyl fencing that looks like wood, and lightweight aluminum fencing that mimics cast iron. Imaginative designers drape chains from concrete posts to mark boundaries, attach multicolored birdhouses to pickets made of slab wood, use unusual materials like sheets of galvanized steel or discarded crates, and otherwise employ innovative ideas for their garden fences. Others grow ivy on their chain link fences, turning them into lush walls of greenery. Classic or one of a kind, an enclosure or a suggestion of one, a fence brings order to the garden.

Fernery

Ferns occur throughout the world, with the preponderance of species in the tropics. They are among the most ancient of plants, originating about 360 million years ago.

In the 1830s, Great Britain was gripped with pteridomania, also known as Fern Fever. It was not quite the madness of Tulipmania, the tulip bulb craze that swept the Netherlands in the seventeenth century; vast sums of money were not speculated on individual ferns. But it does seem everyone caught Fern Fever: wealthy land owners, small lease holders, farmers, young women, professionals. No one was immune; everybody wanted them. Ferns were pretty. They were easy to grow. And they were thought to be a particularly appropriate horticultural hobby for girls, as their reproductive organs, unlike flowers, are not readily apparent. The fern craze spread to other parts of Europe and to the United States.

Collectors spent their leisure hours digging ferns in the woods and hedgerows. They organized expeditions and went out in groups. In addition to local ferns, those who could afford it purchased tender ferns imported from tropical climates.

Of course, if you were going to amass hundreds of ferns, you needed a place to keep them. And so, the fernery was conceived. There were three main places for a fernery: in the house, in a conservatory, or in the garden.

Growing a few ferns in the parlor was the easiest and most prevalent way to have ferns. Early houseplant ferns included maidenhair ferns, sword ferns, and holly ferns. By the 1890s, Boston ferns, a sword fern mutation, had become ubiquitous. Ferns were grown in terra-cotta flowerpots, in planters fashioned from coconut shells, or in iron urns. A whole collection might be grown in

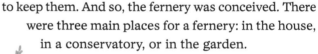

a Wardian case, forerunner to the modern terrarium. Since ferns do not require much light, they thrived in dim Victorian dining rooms and parlors.

Those with large collections of exotic ferns kept them under glass to protect them from winter cold. This could be in a conservatory attached to the house, or in a separate, heated greenhouse. The space might be filled with a variety of ferns or shared with other houseplants such as abutilons, palms, or jasmine. Often a fountain or small pool and a place to sit were included.

Outdoor ferneries could hold more specimens than indoor accommodations, so they proliferated during the Fever. Also called (less colorfully) fern gardens, they could easily be created in a wooded, shaded spot on the property. It was beneficial if there was a stream nearby and a mossy, fallen tree trunk or two. A waterfall was considered very desirable. If shade was not naturally available, a shade house could be made of lattice.

Shirley Hibberd, a nineteenth-century British gardener and writer called the "father of amateur gardening," who preceded William Robinson in advocating something other than carpet bedding, wrote enthusiastically about ferneries in his book, *Rustic Adornments for Homes of Taste.* He later expanded to an entire book devoted to the topic. Hibberd offered several suggestions, including making a bower from the sticks of a brush pile, and mounding a pile of rock and construction debris with leaf mold and compost.

These are foliage gardens at their best.

Though Fern Fever abated more than a hundred years ago, ferneries continue to appeal to gardeners on all but the coldest continents. A fern garden is attractive, has a long season, including winter interest, and can beautify a troublesome, damp and dark corner. These are foliage gardens at their best. Today's fernery might have a mass of one type of fern, or a variety of ferns. It can include ostrich ferns, with fronds up to six feet long; cinnamon ferns, native to much of North America and China; the ethereal ghost fern; or, climate permitting, one of the tropical tree ferns.

No longer the purview of Victorian fussiness, ferneries can be found in sleek concrete and steel outdoor spaces as well as suburban backyards and country gardens.

Fire

People cooked outdoors before they cooked indoors. In warm climates, even after cooking moved into the house, cooks enjoyed the benefits of cooking outdoors during the hottest months. Early bread ovens were set outside, often serving an entire village. Colonial housewives kept a summer kitchen apart from the house. The smokehouse was outside. Italians have long enjoyed baking their pizza in outdoor ovens made of stone or clay. Fire has been in the garden a long, long time.

In the 1930s and 1940s, do-it-yourselfers built fieldstone and sometimes brick or cinder block fireplaces from plans in magazines such as *Popular Mechanics*. A typical fieldstone outdoor fireplace (made of stones gathered on the property) had a chimney in the back, a grill in the front, and burned wood or charcoal briquets.

Charcoal briquettes, pillow-shaped lumps of charcoal, were invented by chemistry professor Orin Stafford and patented in 1923. At the time, Henry Ford wanted to find a use for the wood waste created in the timberlands he had purchased from his friend Edward G. Kingsford to supply wood for his Model Ts. Charcoal briquets (Ford shortened the spelling) were the answer. Thomas Edison designed a factory to produce the charcoal and Ford began selling charcoal briquets and grills in his car dealerships.

In 1951, an employee of the Weber Brothers Metal Works, which manufactured steel buoys, made a grill for himself that was essentially a large buoy cut in half. The Weber Grill was born. By the 1960s, cast iron hibachis and portable steel charcoal and gas grills were in backyards all over America. The gas grill was set up on a patio or next to a deck and though easy and efficient for cooking, and very popular, not much attention was given to the aesthetics of the appliance or how it related to the garden.

Those early grills have evolved into elaborate, gleaming stainless steel affairs. There are also enameled ceramic "eggs" for deep frying, and of course the original Weber Grill. But the hearth has also returned to the backyard, integrated into the garden as part of the decor.

Chimeneas, bottle-like outdoor terra-cotta fireplaces, with a long history in Mexico, appeared in California and the Southwest and spread to the rest of the country. Made of the same clay as flowerpots, they complement a garden.

Originally for cooking and warmth, they are now used to burn aromatic wood or candles. Chimeneas made of cast iron or aluminum are also available, and sturdier than those made of traditional clay.

Firepits, custom built of stone or brick, or premade of iron or copper, are set on pea gravel or pavers and ringed with benches or Adirondack chairs to encourage conversation. They burn wood, charcoal, propane, or alcohol. Twenty-first-century versions of those 1930s fireplaces, made of stone, faux stone, or brick, are offered finished or as kits. They are set at one end of a metal-roofed pavilion or built onto a terrace. Like firepits, they are as much a place to gather as to cook.

For cooking, we see outdoor pizza and bread ovens. These can be handmade of clay, similar to ancient bread ovens, constructed of firebrick, or purchased whole. Rustic and charming, they incorporate well into various garden styles.

Today's outdoor kitchens, far more glamorous than those of our foremothers, now include sinks, cabinets, grills, ovens, refrigerators, fireplaces, tables, and chairs. Roofed, or partially roofed, and usually with a hardscape floor, they are without walls and open to the rest of the garden.

With gardeners embracing flame amidst their flowers, we now see gardens based on the classic four elements: earth, wind, fire, and water.

Flowerpot, Container, Planter

One of the most versatile components of a garden is a planting container. An entire garden can be planted in containers, or containers can be used as accents and focal points. Planted pots can be plunged into a border to add extra color or to fill in gaps. They can divide their time between the house in winter and the deck in warm weather. Containers can be moved about the garden. They provide an opportunity for experimentation with new plants and plant combinations, offering style and flexibility.

Planters are made of various materials such as ceramic, wood, metal, plastic, fiberglass, resin, concrete, tufa, coco fiber, and for grow bags, fabric. Many gardeners delight in using found and repurposed objects such as Italian olive oil cans, leaky row boats, iron cauldrons, or whiskey barrels cut in half. But for much of gardening history, the primary material for garden containers was terra-cotta: fired clay.

Terra-cotta flowerpots depicted on the walls of Egyptian tombs are identical to the classic eighteenth-century flowerpots made by English country potters. Flared, they are the perfect example of form following function. Flowerpots with straight sides, the base narrower than the rim, enable the plant to be removed easily without damage to the roots. Removing a pot-bound plant from a curvaceous pot, or from a pot with a rim that turns inward or is narrower than the base, often requires either smashing the pot, or cutting the roots. With a flared pot, even pot-bound roots can be slipped out.

Potters have been making and gardeners have been using ceramic flowerpots for millennia. Roman gardeners put pots on their windowsills and roofs, in their courtyards and peristyles. They used them for propagating trees and shrubs. Persians punctuated their magnificent formal gardens with terra-cotta pots. The

Florentine potter Luca della Robbia, whose work was in great demand and later imitated, decorated the exteriors of his pots with graceful sprigs and swags of fruit, leaves, and flowers. Pots were important features in Renaissance gardens.

Beginning in the seventeenth century, wealthy Europeans built orangeries to protect their delicate imported citrus trees during the winter. They outfitted their orangeries with very large flowerpots, which they moved out into the garden after all danger of frost had passed. Most of these pots were ceramic, but André le Nôtre created wooden boxes for the orange trees in Louis XIV's collection at Versailles. These iconic planters became known as Versailles Planter Boxes.

With the increased production of plate glass, greenhouses became practical and the horticultural trade burgeoned. Potters made millions of flowerpots to satisfy the needs of indoor and outdoor gardens. They standardized their wares by the weight of the clay before it was thrown on the wheel. Pot styles included seed pans, thimbles, long Toms, and flowerpots large and small.

During the Industrial Revolution, the manufacture of clay flowerpots was mechanized and no longer required potters working at their wheels. These flowerpots looked like the clay pots we are familiar with today. Country potters continued to make pots by hand in England, France, and the United States for another hundred years, offering strawberry pots and hanging planters in the U.S. By the 1960s, the nursery trade had fully embraced lightweight, mass-produced plastic pots, greatly diminishing the demand for clay pots.

A benefit of clay planters is that they are porous, allowing the pots and roots to breathe, which keeps them cooler in the hot sun. The disadvantages are that they are not frost-proof and dry out quickly. This was addressed by using other, nonporous materials before the advent of plastic. Ornate lead cisterns, urns, vases, and planters were in vogue on large English estates in the seventeenth and eighteenth centuries. Eleanor Coade created a secret frost-proof stoneware (high-fired clay) around 1770, and, supplying estates with statues and flowerpots, became wealthy. Tuscan potters, who have been potting in Impruneta (a community in Florence, Italy) for centuries, are blessed with an unusual local clay rich in iron and calcium. Fired to higher temperatures than other flowerpots, clay pots made there are reliably frost-proof. Concrete and stone composite planters also resist frost and gained popularity in the Victorian era.

All containers for growing plants need drainage holes so that the plants do not become waterlogged. However, gardeners have long known that if they place a pot with drainage holes inside a pot or container without holes—a jardiniere—and add a wick, they can slow the drying process and water less often. Today, there are many self-watering planters with an interior well on the market.

Planters can hold a single plant, such as a topiary or small shrub, a single species massed for maximum impact, or a carefully orchestrated combination of plants of complimentary colors and textures. They can be planted with perennials or annuals and changed during the growing year. Growing a plant in a pot, sometimes as a child, is often a gardener's first introduction to the wondrous world of horticulture.

Focal Point

A focal point directs the viewer's gaze by drawing attention to itself and giving the eye a place to rest before taking in the entirety of a garden. It helps the viewer read the landscape. A well-placed focal point can also divert attention from an eyesore. Without focal points, the eye darts around the garden, trying to take in everything, often at great speed.

Large gardens benefit from several focal points, or major and minor focal points, but too many focal points become a distraction. Usually, only one focal point is visible at a time. A cluster of objects can be grouped to form a vignette as focal point, or to lead the eye from a lesser focal point to the greater.

A statue, a bench, a pot or urn, an ornament such as a birdbath, a small building, a stone bust on a plinth—any object the gardener fancies—can be a focal point. It can be an expensive objet d'art, a rusty antique, or a homemade folly. The treasured item is highlighted and the garden is focused.

Specimen plants also make excellent focal points, as long as they look good year-round and are disease resistant. A weeping willow arched over a pond is a classic use of a tree as focal point.

The eye is drawn to visual lines, so placing the focal point at the end of an axis or allée, or the path between double borders, enhances the effect. A focal point placed within a richly planted border adds drama and excitement. Most designers prefer to site a focal point a third or two-thirds of the way down a border rather than at the midpoint, to give a sense of energy.

Author George Plumptre, who has studied the history and placement of ornaments in gardens, points out in his book, *Garden Ornament*, that a time-proven way to make an object a focal point is to work with the light and shadows along the sightline. He suggests that light followed by the shadows cast by a tree or arch (and beyond that, the ornament bathed in a pool of light) lends anticipation and mystery. The eye is drawn to the journey and rewarded with the object.

Many lovely gardens do not have focal points, but a well-thought-out focal point or points adds depth and pleasure to the garden experience, as well as focus, bringing clarity to the garden's story.

Folly

A folly is an extravagant garden building constructed to suggest it is something other than the whimsical decoration it actually is. Purposely built, it might appear to be a mysterious and crumbling castle ruin or a classic ancient temple with Doric columns. Follies echoed Egyptian, Turkish, Chinese, Greek, and Roman architecture. At their peak in England during the eighteenth century, they reflected the cultures and antiquities that the British encountered as they conducted trade throughout the world and administered their empire.

Chinoiserie, or faux Chinese follies, such as the ten-story Great Pagoda at Kew designed by Sir William Chambers in 1762 and the Chinese House at Stowe built by William Kent in 1738, were widely admired, though their designers made no attempt at authenticity. There was also no attempt at thematic unity; follies were meant to spark delighted surprise and, through their associations with distant lands and times, conversation. The same garden might include temples, "ruined" arches, a pyramid, and a pagoda scattered throughout the landscape for the enjoyment of strolling guests.

Follies were meant to spark delighted surprise.

In the United States, Frederick Law Olmstead and Calvert Vaux designed a schist and granite folly for Central Park. Completed in 1869, it was an imposing Gothic-Romanesque structure meant to evoke the ruins of a medieval citadel. Known as Belvedere Castle, its playful uselessness was too much for city authorities, who turned the interior into exhibit space and a weather station.

Not All Folly & Games

There is also a dark side to the story of follies. During the worst months of the first Irish famine in 1740–1741, Katherine Conolly, widow of the wealthiest man in Ireland, put the starving local peasants to work building an elaborate multi-arched stone folly festooned with stone pineapples and eagles, and topped with an obelisk. They also built an astonishing corkscrew-shaped barn for grain, known as the Wonderful Barn, on her estate. She believed people would become lazy if she gave them food outright and so made them work for it. Similarly, during the more famous Potato Famine of 1845, the British government and the local gentry kept the malnourished peasants too busy to revolt by having them build useless follies like roads to nowhere and purposeless stone towers. Together these are all known as the Famine Follies and though built under cruel and dire circumstances, they remain striking in their beauty.

Gardeners who do not have an antique folly on their property can order a folly kit or folly plans from various commercial enterprises. On a more modest level than stone or brick ruins, but follies nonetheless, are whimsical American garden decor additions of the last half-century, such as faux water wells with roofs, rope, and bucket, or small windmills that turn in the wind but generate nothing but passing interest.

Foundation Planting

Though people have often gardened close to their houses, foundation plantings as we know them are a modern phenomenon. During the Arts and Crafts Movement, designers began to tie a house into its surrounding landscape with shrubs, small trees, vines, and terraces, eschewing the expansive lawns of the landscape movement that swept right up to the doors and windows of the house. In the Victorian era, new house foundations protruded higher out of the ground than earlier houses, leading many homeowners to hide or camouflage their foundations with plantings. By the 1930s, foundation plantings were common. Cinder block had come into widespread use for foundation construction, rather than the stone or brick of the past. By the 1970s, poured concrete foundations dominated.

If the Victorians thought their high brick foundations were unsightly, they would have been horrified at the appearance of modern cinder block or poured concrete foundations. With the building boom that followed World War II, and the spread of suburban developments packed with thousands of ranch, split-level, and Cape Cod houses, each with a monolithic gray foundation (or in mild zones, a slab), builders standardized plantings to hide them. They planted four to six evergreen shrubs lined up in a row on each side of the front door. This style is still seen today, often overgrown, with too-tall shrubs that block windows, cutting off air and light.

They echo the architecture of the house and tie it to the larger garden.

It's not that garden writers didn't plead for something better. Leonard H. Johnson published a whole book on the topic in 1927, *Foundation Planting*, in which he advocated a mix of deciduous and evergreen shrubs. *The Woman's Home Companion Garden Book*, published in 1947, told its readers that the planting should be "subordinate to the architecture" and warned of the "disaster" of "bad" foundation planting.

Today, we see foundation plantings that are welcoming gardens. They echo the architecture of the house and tie it to the larger garden, set the tone for the rest of the yard, and yes, hide the ugly concrete foundation. They are a mix of plant elements, deciduous and evergreen, with something of interest for each season. The bed can curve out into the lawn and line the entry walk. Often, the foundation planting extends around all sides of the house. Symmetry is optional, depending upon whether the front of the house itself is symmetrical.

There are several special considerations for foundation plantings. At maturity, they need to be far enough away from the house to allow room for maintenance. Five feet is recommended. They should not have roots that can disturb the foundation or any pipes that extend from it. The area under the eaves receives little moisture from rain and can be very dry. Snow can slide off the roof, especially a metal roof, and hit the plants with force.

With aluminum, vinyl, or fiber cement board siding, it is now possible to cover a foundation so that it is indiscernible from the house, leading some builders to believe foundation plantings are no longer required. However, except for period houses for which you want an authentic landscape, foundation plantings are desirable. They lend warmth and interest and connect the house to the garden.

Furniture

Before houses, before gardens, long before the invention of writing, our prehistoric ancestors rested at some point during their day or in the evening on a boulder or fallen tree. Thus, we can say that the outdoor bench preceded the invention of indoor furniture.

Ancient Middle Eastern and Mediterranean peoples relaxed on benches, chairs, and chaises set in the shade of their grape arbors. They dined alfresco in courtyards and gardens. Greek and later Roman philosophers and scholars expounded from the cool built-in stone benches of the exedrae. Stone garden benches were excavated in Pompeii.

Chinese gardeners at first sat on stools made from logs, but over a thousand years ago, they turned to glazed ceramic stools. These stools, which have a drum-like appearance, were fired to very high temperatures in enormous wood-burning kilns, making them impervious to rain and snow. The medieval gardens of Europe featured turf seats formed from earth, planted with chamomile, thyme, or other herbs. During the Renaissance, gardeners looked back at the classical world and took inspiration from the marble benches of Greece and Rome.

In the nineteenth century, wicker, rattan, and wrought and cast iron became popular materials for outdoor furniture. The use of cast iron, which is made in molds, brought furniture with fancy designs incorporating vines, grapes, flowers, and curlicues to a widespread audience. Similar furniture is now available in lighter weight, rustproof cast aluminum.

Wicker or woven chairs have been known since ancient Egyptian times. In the mid-nineteenth century, Cyrus Wakefield gathered the rattan that was used as packing material for ship cargoes and recycled what was seen as waste into furniture. As the twentieth century dawned, wicker furniture moved onto the porch, into the greenhouse, and into the garden. Today, natural wicker furniture is supplemented with synthetic wicker, which can better withstand the elements.

Twig or rustic furniture has gone in and out of style for centuries. Often hand-made from materials found on-site, it is constructed of bent wood, such as willow, or sticks that are nailed, such as hickory sticks. In the early eighteenth century, the English encountered Chinese landscape gardens and their fantastical twig furniture. As their own landscape movement swept across the land, the English embraced what they perceived as the naturalness of twig or rustic furniture (and buildings). Twig furniture was next embraced in the back-to-nature movement of the late nineteenth century, with the rise of summer camps, and again, during the Depression years of the twentieth century. More durable versions have been made of metal and even ceramics!

The iconic Adirondack chair also came out of the back-to-nature movement. It was designed in 1903 by Thomas Lee, who had a vacation home on the shores of

Lake Champlain. He hired a local carpenter to make the chairs for him during the winter, in time for his return. Unbeknownst to Lee, the carpenter patented and sold the design under his own name. The chairs, originally made of eleven planks, are remarkably comfortable with arms wide enough to hold a drink. Today, in addition to wood Adirondack chairs, there are versions made of synthetics.

It is unclear who designed the first picnic table with table and benches constructed as one unit. There were patents for similar tables in the early years of the twentieth century. In 1922, the National Park Service issued technical drawings in *Table for Public Auto Camp* for the table we know today. Though meant for public use, the tables, easily constructed by the average do-it-yourselfer, moved into the suburban backyard.

The second half of the twentieth century saw folding plastic-webbed chairs and chaise lounges made of tubular aluminum come into style. These were accompanied by stamped-steel motel or clam-back chairs, along with tables, chairs, benches, and chaise lounges made of redwood, cedar, teak, and later sustainable tropical woods. Glass-topped tables, brightly colored bistro tables, resin chairs, and seating with deep, waterproof cushions followed.

Benches are the piece of furniture most symbolic of gardens. Placed as focal points or in a secluded corner or along a path, benches are as much about the suggestion of repose as actual repose. They lead the visitor to imagine for a moment what it would be to linger awhile in the garden.

Garden benches can be made of stone, stone composites, concrete, wood, or metal. They can be as grand as the hand-carved oak bench designed by Edwin Lutyens, widely imitated and reproduced, or as humble as a bench made from three pine planks. Stone benches lend an air of permanence and antiquity to a garden.

Today's gardener can choose furniture from the styles and materials of the past plus a host of new materials and designs. With choices that complement the style of the house and garden, and thought given to placement, furniture can greatly enhance the garden experience.

Garden benches can be . . . as grand as the hand-carved oak bench designed by Edwin Lutyens . . . or as humble as a bench made from three pine planks.

Garden Retreat: Pavilion, Summerhouse, Caravan

Though gardens themselves offer respite from the work day and domestic pressures, the addition of a special structure within the garden gives welcome and privacy. It can be a place to chat with friends and family or a place for solitude.

A summerhouse is a structure set apart from the main house for use in warm weather. With screened or latticed openings to catch breezes, a summerhouse provides cool shelter from the summer sun. Square or rectangular, it can be large enough for gatherings, or small and intimate enough for a single chair. It is a pleasant spot for dining, reading, or taking a nap.

Rotating summerhouses were popular in England from the Victorian era until the 1920s. In northern Europe, they were used

A rotating summerhouse could turn toward or away from the sun, depending upon whether one wanted warmth or shade.

in sanitoriums for tuberculosis patients to "take the air" during their cure. They were built on an iron mechanism which was placed on a flat, paved surface in the garden. The front of a rotating summerhouse could be opened and closed with folding doors. Windows were glazed. A rotating summerhouse could turn toward or away from the sun, depending upon whether one wanted warmth or shade. Restored and reproduction rotating summerhouses are available today.

A pavilion ("ramada" in the American Southwest) is also an outdoor structure, but is less enclosed than a summerhouse. It consists of sturdy uprights made of wooden beams or masonry and a pitched roof. Some have a partial open wall of spindles. It might have a built-in floor or be set on a stone or concrete base. Pavilions offer a shady spot for picnic tables, a hammock, chairs, and benches. They are popular with volunteer fire departments and town parks as they are usually large enough to accommodate quite a few people. They also work well in a garden, sometimes doubling as a carport in winter.

Shepherd's huts, now popular in gardens, had their origins in the nineteenth century. Durable and sturdy, with windows on both sides and four wheels, these huts came from southern England. Here the soils were thin and chalky and required manure to be productive. Farmers kept flocks of sheep to graze and, more importantly, fertilize their fields. The sheep were confined to a single area with hurdles, and then when that area was grazed, the sheep were moved to another area, leaving the field well fertilized. A shepherd stayed with the sheep. He slept and ate in his shed. Here he kept his tools, food, and medicines. There was a small stove, shelves, and a bed.

Antique and reproduction caravans and shepherd's huts are now found more often in gardens than on the road. They make a charming retreat in any weather, serve as a place for extra guests to sleep, and bring whimsey and history to the garden.

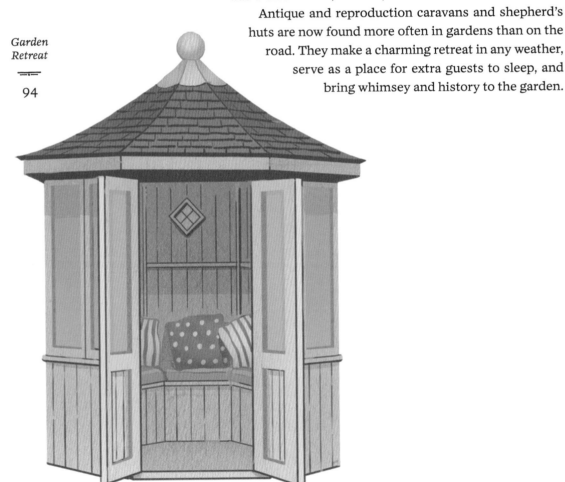

The Embellished Retreat

Gypsy caravans have found popularity as garden retreats, especially in the UK. Nineteenth-century Romani people and carnival workers liked to travel in ornate, brightly painted and gilded wagons pulled by horses. The wagons were made in five styles:

- **Bowtop**, with a wooden frame and rounded plain canvas covered top insulated with felt, easy to hide and difficult to tip over
- **Burton** or **Showman's** caravan, with equal-size wheels and a long body with vertical sides
- **Ledge**, with a larger rear wheel, vertical lower wall, and upper ledge
- **Openlot**, a bowtop with open ends, protected only by a curtain
- **Reading**, with large rear wheels and sloping sides.

The children's author Roald Dahl, fascinated with Romani culture, had a colorful blue caravan in his garden where he secluded himself to write. He wrote about it in his book, *Danny, the Champion of the World,* enchanting generations of readers.

Gate

The word gate comes from the Old Norse *gat* for opening, related to Old Saxon *gat,* for eye of a needle, and Dutch *gat* for hole or breach. Today, the Oxford English Dictionary defines gate as a "hinged barrier used to close an opening in a wall, hedge, or fence." Medieval European garden gates kept animals from entering the enclosed garden and wreaking havoc. Early American towns and villages generally required homeowners to erect a fence within six months or so of building their house, in order to contain livestock. Their gates were simple wooden affairs similar to the fences.

Throughout history, as cultures acquired leisure and economic stability, gates gained an aesthetic role equal to their utilitarian role and came to be as much a symbol of welcome, conviviality, and status as protection against unwanted visitors. By the end of the seventeenth century, iron gates came into vogue in the UK. The Georgian and Federal Periods in the United States, the Arts and Crafts Movement, and the Victorian era enjoyed a flowering of architecturally harmonious gates. Chinese-inspired Chippendale-style gates and Gothic gates came into vogue. White picket fences with simple picket gates, often topped by an arbor, were widespread during the late colonial period of the United States. In twentieth-century shelter magazines, they were synonymous with suburban harmony. "Over the garden gate" implied a gossipy conversation between neighbors.

A gate can suggest mystery, romance, drama, rusticity, or sophistication.

A gate should reflect the style of the house and garden it serves. Depending upon the gardener's intent, a gate can suggest mystery, romance, drama, rusticity, or sophistication. It can offer a framed glimpse of the garden, or completely block sight of a secret garden until the gate, more like a door, is opened.

Moon gates, a feature of Chinese gardens, are round openings or passageways in a garden wall. Traditionally the purview of wealthy, fourth-century Chinese landowners and made of stone or stone and tile, they now grace gardens throughout the world, particularly Bermuda. In the 1860s a Bermudan sailor who had seen moon gates in China constructed one of stone in his island garden. Soon other islanders were building moon gates and the Chinese origins were lost in memory for more than half a century, as the garden feature became known as a Bermuda Moon Gate. In addition to stone, modern moon gates in the United States and the UK are constructed of wood and various metals.

The Japanese *torii* gate is historically the entrance to a Shinto shrine. Passing through the gate represents leaving the ordinary behind and entering the sacred. Usually painted red, these graceful wood-framed openings, absent a shrine, serve as garden entrances in America and elsewhere, notably Butchart Gardens in Canada.

Gates in western gardens can be single-swing, double-swing, sliding, lift-up, or accordion. The single- and double-swing are the most prevalent for gardens. In 1886, the author and designer Frank J. Scott warned his readers that gates must be sturdy. In his book, *The Art of Beautifying Suburban Home Grounds*, he pointed out that there is no stopping children from swinging on gates, so they best be constructed to withstand such abuse.

Gates must be immediately apparent so visitors can easily find them. This is accomplished by making the gate posts more substantial than the fence, or by varying the height of the gate with the fence, hedge, or wall. Posts might be built of brick and topped with urns. They might be made of wood or iron and sport knobs, finials, or caps.

Today's gardener has a plethora of styles to draw upon when choosing a gate. A gate gives a sense of enclosure and expectancy and enhances the garden even if not needed for security. Left ajar, a garden gate says welcome, please enter.

Gazebo

Outdoor structures for dining, viewing, and capturing breezes have graced gardens almost as long as there have been gardens. Egyptians, Greeks, Romans, Persians, Chinese—all the great gardeners of the past—added structures to their gardens to enhance their outdoor experience. Though we might retrospectively think of some of these structures as gazebos, the word itself did not appear in English until the mid-eighteenth century, when it was used by a British garden writer to describe an outdoor structure in a Chinese garden.

Gazebos as we know them today were popular throughout the Middle Ages in Europe, particularly in monastic gardens. By the eighteenth century, they also embellished gardens in the United States. During the first half of the nineteenth century, gazebos were ubiquitous status symbols in the gardens of middle and upper classes who were enjoying increased income and leisure.

A gazebo is an open structure with a roof and floor. It is enclosed with airy full or half walls of lattice, spindles, or chinoiserie-style openwork. It is most often octagonal or hexagonal. It can be ornate, with a double roof, cupula, and carved brackets, or more rustic, constructed of peeled logs or cedar. Construction is generally of wood, but brick, stones, and metal are also used. Today even vinyl is available.

Gazebos as we know them today were popular throughout the Middle Ages in Europe, particularly in monastic gardens.

A gazebo can be freestanding or incorporated into a wall. It should be far enough from the house to feel separate, yet carefully integrated into the garden. The openings should frame pleasant views of the garden and let breezes waft through. Many gazebos have a built-in bench around the perimeter, but movable furniture offers more flexibility.

After wire window screens were introduced to the market by a nineteenth-century sieve maker in Connecticut, screens became available for gazebos and summerhouses. Guests could enjoy the evening garden without fear of mosquitoes.

The words gazebo and summerhouse are sometimes used interchangeably, but a summerhouse is generally rectangular or oblong, and might have partially closed walls. A belvedere, also similar to a gazebo, is built specifically for enjoying a view.

It can be freestanding like a gazebo, but it can also be part of the upper story of a house, or tower. Belvederes were a popular feature in the gardens of seventeenth-century Italy, France, and England.

Many of the wood gazebos and outbuildings that graced nineteenth-century gardens fell into disrepair by the 1940s and collapsed in ruin. They were replaced with patios and decks. Today, however, it is not unusual to see a prefabricated gazebo whizzing down the road on a flatbed truck as it is delivered to someone's backyard. Gazebos, festooned with hanging planters, furnished with cushioned chairs and, if space allows, a hammock, are once again a fashionable garden feature. They are placed in the garden in addition to a deck or patio.

Patio stones, cinder blocks, and concrete footings are options for the foundation. Building permits, even for prefabs, are usually necessary. However, once installed, a gazebo is a wonderful focal point and adds a new dimension to enjoying the garden.

Geometry, Mathematics

The "Gardiner," John Evelyn wrote, must have more than a "Superficial Skill in the Mathematicks." He explained that the gardener must be able to calculate rectangles, squares, and triangles and measure accurately using an "Instrument," lest all sorts of "Errours & extraordinary Expences" befall.

Geometry has underlain gardens from the earliest Egyptian grids to the Persian *chahar bagh*; from the gardens of the Italian Renaissance to, perhaps surprisingly, the picturesque gardens of the eighteenth century. Seen and unseen mathematics guides design.

The chahar bagh is based on four quadrants divided by paths or water courses. The quadrants represent the four gardens of heaven in the Qur'an. This quadripartite garden design, four square or rectangular garden beds within a larger enclosed square or rectangle, connected with cruciform paths, appears in gardens throughout history and throughout the world. This layout, sometimes in multiples, was used in medieval monastery gardens, early American dooryard gardens, and modern herb gardens. It was used by the Moors in Spain and in formal English gardens. A variation is to divide the garden into quadrants on the diagonal, creating an X or Saint Andrew's Cross.

Related is the quincunx, with four points at the corners and one in the center. The quincunx is a time-honored pattern for orchards as it gives access to each tree, makes efficient use of the land, and encourages pollination.

Garden layouts incorporate squares, rectangles, circles, and triangles to organize the space. Think of the circular garden around a fountain or birdbath, crossed by paths coming from four evenly spaced sides. Think of the rectangular deck, the square foot garden, or square planter.

Geometry also guides the garden axis. Axes are made with straight lines leading from one place, say the front door, to another, perhaps a bench. An axis leads the eye and pulls the visitor on a journey. An axis may be crossed by a secondary axis, also straight, at a right angle. To give an axis the illusion of greater length than it really is, the gardener narrows it at the farther end.

An allée, which is also straight, relies on planting symmetry. Plants line both sides of the allée, placed in opposite pairs. Both axes and allées require careful measurement to construct. They are also both what artists and designers call leading lines. A leading line leads the eye. A curved path, while not an axis, can be a leading line.

Many gardens that at first glance seem outside the bounds of math rely on the golden ratio (sometimes called the divine proportion) and, related, the Fibonacci sequence. The golden ratio and the Fibonacci sequence were discovered by the brilliant mathematician Leonardo de Pisa, called Fibonacci or Son of Bonacci.

Based on the golden ratio, the short sides of a golden rectangle are .618 of the length of the long side. This is a ratio much beloved by artists because designs that follows it are naturally pleasing to the eye. It occurs throughout nature. It is an effective guide in laying out a garden.

Numbers in the Fibonacci sequence, which are related to the golden ratio for mathematical reasons we will not delve into here, are 0, 1, 1, 2, 3, 5, 8, 13, 21, 34 and so on: the sum of the two preceding numbers. Instinctively, many gardeners plant in groups of three or five because it looks good. The golden ratio can also be used to determine heights of plants.

The rule of thirds, used in many artistic disciplines such as photography and painting, and also intuitively by a gardener "with a good eye," divides a garden scene into thirds horizontally and vertically. Rather than placing a focal point, such as an urn, specimen tree, or if you are Capability Brown, a temple, you place it to the left or right of the center, at the intersection of your imaginary lines, thus creating a pleasing picture.

The geometry of formal gardens is readily apparent and understood. We immediately see the geometry of a parterre or a quadrilateral potager. The math speaks a universal language that soothes and reassures the viewer. The geometry in the garden of curves and informality, while undergirding the layout and also speaking a universal language, is more subtly felt—but speaks to us nevertheless.

Greenhouse, Conservatory, Orangery

"Who loves a garden loves a greenhouse too," the poet William Cowper asserts in his acclaimed free-verse poem, *The Task*. He continues, "Unconscious of a less propitious clime, There blooms exotic beauty, warm and snug." The purpose of a greenhouse is to extend the season or grow plants that one's climate cannot otherwise accommodate. Originally, the words greenhouse and conservatory were synonymous (the great John Evelyn was the first to use either in writing), but today, a greenhouse is generally freestanding and primarily for propagating and growing. A conservatory is often attached to a house and extends into the garden. It is primarily for the display of tender and exotic plants and can include a few chairs or a table.

A greenhouse was discovered at Pompeii, dating from the first century. It had hot-air flues built into the walls and shelves for plants. One wall had either glass or a glass substitute such as transparent mica. The Romans were adept at forcing plants. The first-century Roman writers Columella, Martial, and Seneca all mention greenhouses, with Martial complaining that he had to sleep in a cold room with an open window, while the vines his host grew got a room with a mica window. Seneca bemoaned the excessive luxury of greenhouses; indeed, they were only for the very wealthiest citizens.

It was the introduction of sweet oranges to the cooler countries of Europe that led to the development of greenhouses as we think of them. Moors brought orange trees to Spain in the tenth century. By the late fifteenth or early sixteenth century, the trees were introduced into Italy and Portugal and moved on to France and England, where winters were inhospitable. The first orangeries, built to protect the trees in the winter, were heated sheds, rooms, or cellars. Trees were planted in large terra-cotta pots or wooden tubs and moved outdoors for summer and into the orangery for winter. However, the lack of sunlight and fumes from the fires in the orangeries killed many of the precious trees.

By the last years of the seventeenth century, with the invention of plate glass, large windows were used on the south sides of orangeries. Louis the XIV, who insisted on the biggest and best of everything for his palace and gardens at Versailles, had an enormous orangery built with south-facing windows to house his 1200 potted orange trees and other exotics.

In 1816, John Claudius Loudon invented the flexible wrought iron glazing bar, making all-glass greenhouses possible. Greenhouse mania ensued. In 1851, Sir Joseph Paxton designed the enormous and ornate Crystal Palace, the world's largest glasshouse at the time.

The problem of fumes was solved by using manure and tan bark. Both livestock manure and tan bark, a biproduct of the leather-tanning industry, give off a remarkable amount of heat as they decay. Later, hot water heat and boilers came into use.

The first American greenhouse was built in Boston by Andrew Faneuil around 1737. By the Victorian era, conservatories filled with plants were de rigueur for fashionable members of the upper classes. Mark Twain enjoyed the polygonal conservatory he had included in his 1874 brick Victorian Gothic mansion in Hartford, Connecticut. Extending from the library, and reached through sliding doors, the conservatory had a pointed roof, gravel floor, and bubbling fountain. His friend, the actor William Gillette, included a similar conservatory in the stone castle he built for himself overlooking the Connecticut River. Both conservatories are open to the public today.

A greenhouse was discovered at Pompeii, dating from the first century. It had hot-air flues built into the walls and shelves for plants.

Large estates in England required multiple greenhouses that were kept at different temperatures to provide food for the household and flowers for the house, church, and local floral competitions. These structures produced an abundance of grapes, pineapples, melons, bananas, oranges, and lemons. In his memoir, *Garden Glory: Autobiography of a Gardener*, Ted Humphris describes greenhouses filled with orchids, arum lilies, gardenias, bougainvillea, crotons, caladium, palms, stephanotis, begonias, gloxinia, oleander, sweet violets, camellia, chrysanthemums, datura, dracaenas, cyclamen, fuchsia, and cinerarias, along with those devoted to fruits or starting vegetables.

Today, large growers often use hoop houses, which are quick to erect and cost-effective. Covered with heavy-duty, transparent plastic, they do not last as long as a glasshouse nor are they as attractive, but they are effective.

Traditional greenhouses are widely available for today's gardener. They come in a variety of styles and sizes, with wood, aluminum, or steel frames. The traditional span greenhouse is freestanding with vertical sides. Both roof spans are equal. Barn-like, it can have a knee-wall or glass to the ground. A variation is the three-quarter span, with one span larger than the other. It is positioned against a wall. Similarly, the lean-to greenhouse has one span and is positioned against a wall. The lean-to can also be constructed as a conservatory, open to the house. Less traditional shapes include domes and polygons.

Heat, ventilation, and summer shading must be taken into consideration. Cold or unheated greenhouses are used to extend the garden season. A cold greenhouse can be used to overwinter plants, for alpines, and for early bulbs. With a heating coil beneath the pots or beds, it can be used for propagation. A cool or frost-free greenhouse maintains a minimum night temperature above freezing, and a daytime low temperature of 41–50ºF. In addition to the same uses as a cold greenhouse, it can house frost-tender plants, and be used for some vegetables and flowers. A temperate greenhouse maintains a minimum nighttime temperature of 45ºF and a low daytime temperature of 50–55ºF. It can house a wider range of plants, including houseplants and tropicals. A warm greenhouse has a minimum night temperature of 55ºF and daytime temperatures to 65ºF, warmer if it is also used as a sitting area.

Greenhouses and conservatories should be sited for maximum winter sun. The gardener can tie the house, greenhouse, or conservatory and garden together with walks, terraces, and plants. Inside, the greenhouse can be furnished with shelves, raised beds, benches, pots, and grow bags. A center path is efficient and traditional. The floor can be brick, tile, gravel, or dirt. Conservatories might include furniture for people, such as a metal bistro table and chairs, a fountain or built-in grotto, an unusual rock, or a piece of sculpture.

Whether modest or grand, a greenhouse or conservatory adds excitement and interest to any garden and gives the gardener more time for horticultural pursuits by extending the growing season.

Grotto

A grotto is a small, decorated cave, usually with a water feature. Ancient Greeks and Romans made grottoes in seaside caves to honor the water nymphs they believed resided there. They also made grottoes in their villas and near natural springs, which they furnished with stone statues of nymphs and referred to as nymphaeums. Grottoes were sacred places for contemplation and offered sanctuary from the summer heat.

Beginning in fifteenth-century Italy, there was a renewed interest in grottoes. By the sixteenth century, they enjoyed a revival throughout Europe, becoming very popular in the British Isles in the seventeenth century. If an authentic cave was not available, a gardener would have large rocks moved into place to fabricate one. Entrances were shrouded in mystery and darkness. Inside, they were fantastically decorated with fountains, statues, shells, and artificial stalactites and stalagmites. Interestingly, the word "grotesque" arose during this time, originally meaning "that found in a grotto."

Shell work was often the purview of the women of the house. The Duchess of Richmond and her two oldest daughters spent seven years decorating their grotto. They collected thousands of shells from all over the world which they used to create swags, bows, and cornucopias on the interior walls. They decorated the exterior with fossils and pieces of flint.

The Duchess of Richmond and her two oldest daughters spent seven years decorating their grotto.

The sixteenth-century French potter, Bernard Palissy, known for embellishing his brightly glazed earthenware platters and vases with realistic-looking ceramic lizards, snakes, frogs, and vines, made equally realistic decorations for several grottoes, most famously for the Queen Mother, Catherine de Medici. It was said his ceramic fish were so convincingly made, they appeared to swim.

In the eighteenth century, James Pulham invented a way to manufacture artificial stone which he called Pulhamite. Gardeners could enjoy grottoes and rock gardens even if rocks were not available. This enabled many more gardeners to add grottoes to their estates.

Garden grottoes, built to stimulate emotions and the imagination, were often associated with hermits thought to dwell deep within. With advances in hydraulics, grottoes sometimes included water jokes, and guests were unexpectedly doused. In addition, many small grottoes, some barely larger than a niche, were built as special rooms beneath stairwells and in courtyards. Interestingly, Chinese gardeners also had a fancy for grottoes. Writing in 1026, the statesman Hsi-Ma-Kuang describes one that is remarkably like those in Europe:

> . . . there is a deep grotto, which gets wider the farther one goes, and makes a kind of irregularly-shaped room with an arched ceiling. The light comes in through a somewhat large opening hung round with wild vine and honeysuckle. Rocks serve as seats, one gets protection in the blazing dog-days by going into the alcoves and sitting there. A small stream comes out on one side and fills the hollow of a great stone, and then drops out in little trickles to the floor, winding about in the cracks and fissures till it falls into a reservoir bath. This basin has more depth when it reaches an arch, where it makes a little turn and flows into a pond, which is down at the bottom of the grotto.

Though many European grottoes fell into disrepair, became overgrown, or were destroyed in the late nineteenth and early twentieth centuries, interest in them never entirely disappeared. The garden historian, author, and designer Rosemary Verey, famous for her much-visited garden at Barnsley House, late in life realized her long-held dream of making a grotto. She sought the advice of Diana Reynell, known as the "queen of grotto restorers and makers." Reynell liked to quote Leonardo da Vinci to her clients: "And after having remained at the entry some time, two contrary emotions arose in me, fear and desire—fear of the threatening dark grotto, desire to see whether there were any marvelous thing in it." The grotto she created for Verey in Verey's conservatory was made of stone and shells and featured statuary and three pools. Verey loved her grotto, writing fondly of it in her book, *Making A Garden*.

Vernacular grottoes in backyard gardens, most prevalent in New England and the South, include half-buried claw-foot bathtubs, sunk upright in the earth so the curved end is uppermost, a statue of Mary within. For those without old bathtubs, there are prefabricated grottoes made of cement that the faithful can install in their gardens.

One of the most ambitious twenty-first-century grottoes was built at Longwood Gardens, the du Pont estate, in Pennsylvania. It was constructed of local stone flecked with mica. The Longwood gardeners, who embarked on extensive research before undertaking this large project, describe it as "otherworldly" and "ethereal." It is open to the public.

Waterfall grottoes have become a fashionable complement to in-ground swimming pools. Built of stone or artificial stone, they include a cascade of water that spills over a cave, offering both drama and levity. Swimmers can enter the cave or splash in the shower. Combined with plantings and more rocks, grottoes nicely tie a swimming pool to the surrounding landscape.

Grotto

Ha-Ha

A ha-ha is a ditch that is deep enough and wide enough to be a barrier for livestock, yet does not interrupt the view as a fence or wall would. A ha-ha was the original invisible fence. Early ha-has had a fence or hedge inside at the base. Later, more elaborate examples had one side made of slanted turf, while the opposite side was vertical, usually held in place with a stone or brick retaining wall.

Charles Bridgeman, William Kent, Capability Brown, and other landscape garden designers installed numerous ha-has during the eighteenth century. With a ha-ha in place, the lord of the manor could look out from his windows and see a flock of sheep contentedly grazing in his parklands, without worrying that the sheep would come close to the house and leave droppings on the lawn or nibble the flowers. A ha-ha brought a sense of openness to the vistas while separating formal areas from the meadows, pastures, and woodlands, or even neighboring properties. A ha-ha eliminated the sense of enclosure that had been a key feature of earlier gardens.

Alexander Pope, writing in 1724 about the ha-has in the garden at Stowe House in Buckinghamshire, England, said, "What adds to the beauty of this garden is that it is not bounded by walls, but by a ha-ha, which leaves you the sight of a beautiful woody country, and makes you ignorant how far the high-planted walks extend." The ha-has that so impressed Pope were installed by Bridgeman. Later, Kent took charge, joined by and then followed by Brown who stayed as head gardener until he set out on his own. All three leading landscape gardeners had a hand in the gardens of Stowe.

Horace Walpole, also a fan of ha-has, claimed that the word ha-ha comes from the exclamation of surprise a visitor might emit when suddenly coming upon one: "Ha-ha!" or more aptly, "Ah-ha!" His explanation is disputed by some authorities, however. He also referred to the ha-ha at his estate, Strawberry Hill, as a "sunk fence," saying that it was "a simple enchantment."

A ha-ha is a ditch that is deep enough and wide enough to be a barrier for livestock, yet does not interrupt the view.

Henry Repton, one of the last landscape gardeners of the eighteenth century, employed sunk fences (or a ha!ha! as he also referred to the feature) in his designs, and promoted their use and benefits in his book, *The Art of Landscape Gardening*. He cautioned against half measures or compromises when making a ha-ha: old boundaries must go, and the ha-ha must be straight. The result, however, was "imaginary freedom" in land that was actually subdivided and bounded.

Contemporary gardeners have also discovered that a ha-ha can be a design element itself or inspire one. Charles Jenks has used the ha-ha concept in his landforms at his Garden of Cosmic Speculation in Scotland. Others make more traditional ha-has, a much easier task with today's earth-moving equipment.

Though ha-has are still employed in gardens today, designers must take safety into consideration to prevent unsuspecting visitors from tumbling head first into the bottoms of sunken ditches! Some jurisdictions require that they be made visible, which of course defeats the purpose of this clever contrivance.

Hardscape

Hardscape consists of the non-vegetative materials in a garden, including the paths, terraces, structures, fountains, pools, rills, pavements, driveways, and walls. It can be made of wood, stone, brick, concrete, metal, glass, vinyl, or ceramic. Most designers recommend installing the hardscape before planting, but the budget does not always allow this. Ideally, then, one should at least plan for the hardscaping in the early stages. However, all too often, ten years into a garden, we suddenly realize we must have a pergola or other feature in which we previously had no interest.

Hardscape has been a key element of gardens since unknown ancestors in deepest history set down stepping stones to keep their feet dry. It is the most permanent aspect of the garden, sometimes lasting centuries after the plants have vanished. Archaeologists uncover ancient wells and walkways. A homeowner, digging on her property, might come upon a lost stone terrace or the outline of a summer house. Walls remain long after the borders have reverted to weeds.

Permanence is a feature of hardscape not just over the years, but during each year. Plants change with the seasons, emerge, blossom, go to seed, die back; leaves change color and drop—but the terrace remains unchanged, the walk still leads the way, the potting shed beckons. It is the hardscape we see when winter comes.

Hardscape works with and enhances the softscape—the plants, mulches, and lawns, and the decor, including ornaments and furniture. It is the backbone of the garden.

Though pavement is only one element of hardscaping, it is a foundation of garden design. Of course, gardens exist without any pavement, such as cottage gardens, but most gardens have at least some paving for walks, drives, and perhaps a sitting area. Common paving materials are brick, concrete, fieldstone, cut stone, artificial stone, gravel, mosaic pieces, decomposed granite, and stone dust. Low-growing, creeping plants such as thyme are a favorite to tuck between random stones or pavers, adding scent and texture.

> Hardscape has been a key element of gardens since unknown ancestors in deepest history set down stepping stones to keep their feet dry.

Pervious pavement, which allows rainwater to pass through, has seen increased use in the past fifty years. Open grids made of recycled plastic and infilled with gravel or grass is also gaining in popularity for driveways and walks.

Walls, too, are a key component of hardscaping. They are used to divide or bound garden space, hold back a hillside or slope, act as a barrier to prevent people from falling off a terrace, as protection from foraging livestock and wildlife, and as a background for a border. They are made of stone, brick, cob, adobe or rammed earth, sod, concrete, or a combination of materials—materials that have been used for thousands of years. Walls in areas with frost require footings to keep them from toppling as the ground freezes and thaws.

Stone walls are made of naturally occurring stone and cut stone, laid both with and without mortar. They give a venerable look of age and permanence to the landscape. Local stone usually fits best with the garden as the colors are compatible. When crevices in the wall are filled with soil, a variety of plants can be grown in the pockets, softening the appearance.

Bricks, *from* Jericho to George

Sun-baked clay bricks formed the walls of Jericho almost 10,000 years ago. Fired clay bricks were made as early as 3500 BCE. Today, brick walls grace gardens throughout much of the world. A brick wall no higher than three feet tall can safely be made the width of a single brick. Higher than that, the wall needs to be thicker for stability. To accomplish this, many bricklaying patterns were developed, including Flemish style, with a hollow interior. When King George III instituted a brick tax in England at the end of the eighteenth century, bricklayers developed the sinuous serpentine wall so that fewer bricks were required. As long as the radius of the curve equaled twice the height of the wall, serpentine walls needed only the thickness of one brick. Today, bricks offer many design possibilities, including open work.

Hedge

A hedge is a living wall. It frames the garden. It can provide privacy or screen an unwanted view. Hedges can separate areas of a garden, creating rooms or compartments. They can be planted as windbreaks or barriers to unwanted intruders. Leafy and green, hedges make wonderful backdrops for borders, garden ornaments, and fountains.

There are two types of hedges: formal and informal. Formal hedges are trimmed. Informal hedges are untrimmed. Formal hedges are made of a single species, evergreen or deciduous, such as yew or hawthorn. Informal hedges can be a single species or mixed. Either can be as low as several inches, such as a hedge of lavender in an herb garden or the box of a parterre, or many feet high. The Meikleour Beech Hedge in Scotland, considered the tallest hedge in the world, is ninety-eight feet tall and a third of a mile long. It was planted in 1745.

Evergreen hedges offer winter interest when most of the garden is brown. Throughout the year, they provide privacy and screen out unwanted views. A deciduous hedge is airy and less private, changing with the seasons. Classic and traditional hedging plants include arborvitae, barberry, boxwood, forsythia, hemlock, holly, hornbeam, lilac, privet, and yew.

Typically, formal hedges are eight to ten feet tall, with waist-high hedges often planted across the front of a property. Trimming is done annually for slow-growing hedges, but hedges of fast growers such as privet and honeysuckle require a trim two or three times during the summer in order to look good. A formal hedge is trimmed with flat sides that are wider at the base so that rain and sun can reach the lower branches. The top is trimmed straight across except in snowy areas where the top is somewhat rounded to help prevent damage from the weight of the snow.

Openings such as windows and archways cut into a hedge can offer a glimpse of other parts of the garden or set off a borrowed view. They entice visitors to imagine what lies ahead, drawing them forward. An opening in a hedge on the street side of a property shares parts of the garden with passersby while maintaining a boundary.

Hedges can be embellished with topiary, adding the whimsey of a rabbit or geometry of a clipped ball. An entire hedge can be trimmed as topiary with undulating waves or mounds. The ancient Romans, who loved both topiary and formal hedges, often combined the two at their villa gardens.

Over the centuries, gardeners have invented many tools for the task of keeping a hedge properly trimmed. There were ladders, clippers, sheers, and wooden guides to ensure that the hedge was cut at the proper angle from top to bottom. Today, power tools do the job.

A neglected formal hedge gives the garden an untended and unkempt look. Happily, because they are made of species that take to clipping, neglected and overgrown hedges can often be rejuvenated. Some of the most photographed and intriguing old hedges are the result of long periods of neglect. The Elephant Hedge, planted 400 years ago at Rockingham Palace in the UK, lost its original shape from neglected trimming but is now a wall of billowing shapes in which appear the illusion of elephants. The Dark Hedges in Northern Ireland were planted in the eighteenth century as two parallel beech hedges lining the entrance avenue to the Stuart family's Grace Hill House. Untrimmed, they grew into a dark and mysterious tunnel of twisted trunks.

The Meikleour Beech Hedge in Scotland, considered the tallest hedge in the world, is ninety-eight feet tall and a third of a mile long.

When a new invading blight or disease unexpectedly attacks, such as hemlock woolly adelgid, a beautiful single species hedge that took years to grow can suddenly die. Hemlock woolly adelgid is attacking hemlock hedges in much of the United States, particularly the Northeast, and though there are now defenses against the sucking insect, hedges were lost, especially in the years before the cause was identified. Though hedges often outlast those who planted them by many generations, they are susceptible to heartbreaking ruin.

Informal hedges require only occasional trimming or pruning to remove a dead branch or keep growth in bounds. They take up more room than a formal hedge but require less work. They can be made of a sweep of a single species, such as lilacs, hydrangeas, shrub roses, or a mix. Because they are not trimmed, flowers are often part of their appeal. Informal hedges hark back to the hedgerows that grew between farm fields and pastures from neolithic times and fit nicely in today's informal gardens. They are perfect for the relaxed lifestyle.

Hedges that are a bit airy make the best windbreaks. They diffuse the wind rather than block it, which would subject the trees or shrubs to damage. A windbreak hedge extends wind protection out eight times the height of the hedge.

A hedge is a long-term component of a garden, setting the overall personality and identity. Even when other elements falter or die back naturally in winter, hedges make a garden look like a garden.

Herb Garden

You can tuck a few herbs into the vegetable or flower garden. You can grow them in pots on a windowsill or outside on a deck or terrace. Or you can have an herb garden: a specialty garden dedicated to herbs, usually set within a larger garden.

Herbs are plants with fragrant or savory leaves traditionally used in cooking, medicine, beauty care, and to freshen linens and closets. Though most have flowers, it is often not the flowers that we primarily value. Most herbs require sun and are drought tolerant. Exceptions are herbs such as chervil, which likes some shade, and mint, which prefers moisture.

Herbs have been grown throughout history, with garden writers from ancient Sumer to the present eager to give advice on the use and cultivation of these useful plants. Over 5000 years ago, the Sumerians listed herbs on clay tablets. In China, Shen Nung wrote *Pen Ts'ao*, a long list of herbs and their medical uses, in 3000 BCE. An illustrated ancient Egyptian herbal, the *Ebers Papyrus,* which survives from the first century BCE, lists nearly a thousand herbal medicines.

Two ancient Greek physicians and herbalists—Dioscorides, physician to the Roman army, and Galen, court physician to Marcus Aurelius—wrote herbals that were translated into Latin and referenced for centuries. Monks relied on handwritten copies of these ancient texts to understand how best to use their herbs in treating themselves and the sick they tended. We know from illustrated manuscripts and other documents that these monastic physic gardens were raised, rectangular beds and paths, and were enclosed. In some monasteries, each monk would have a small physic garden attached to his tiny abode. With the invention of the printing press, both Dioscorides's and Galen's books became widely available beyond the monasteries.

Herbs were strewn on the floors of homes in the Middle Ages, sewn into sachets, tucked into hats.

For centuries, home gardeners have grown herbs for cooking, for remedies to various ailments, and for other household uses. Herbs were strewn on the floors of homes in the Middle Ages, sewn into sachets, tucked into hats. Herbs were associated with myths, folklore, festivals, and, since the days of monastic physic gardens, individual saints. Sadly, some women who were particularly skilled with herbs were suspected of witchcraft.

In 1653, Nicholas Culpeper published his extensive and much-reprinted *Complete Herbal*. His goal was to make herbal knowledge accessible to everyone and, though he died at a young age, he succeeded. However, as medicine became the provenance of specially trained physicians, herbs waned in importance. It was no longer necessary for every housewife to be able to identify herbs or grow them in her dooryard, though it was necessary longer in colonial America, where households had to be self-sufficient. Early Americans called herbs "simples".

Adelma Simmons, who founded Caprilands Herb Farm in 1929, in Coventry, Connecticut, helped popularize herb gardens in the twentieth century. Celebrity chefs, movie stars, and busloads of gardeners flocked to the herb gardens that surrounded her late-eighteenth-century farmhouse. She offered herbal lunches coupled with lively lectures on herbs. Dressed in a cape and tiny cap, she was always willing to autograph her books for visitors. Magazines and newspapers adored her and by the 1970s she and her herb farm were famous.

Today, herb gardens are traditionally symmetrical, made with brick or gravel paths between beds, perhaps a sundial or birdbath in the center. Stylistically, they nod to the layout of monastic physic gardens which influenced herb garden design through the years, including early American herb gardens. Knot gardens and parterres work well for traditional herb gardens.

Yet there is no horticultural reason to follow tradition. An herb garden planted between the rungs of a ladder that has been laid on the ground makes an interesting conversation piece. Herbs can be planted according to color, such as all silver and gray. A garden can feature herbs that make good dyes, or can be used for wreaths or sachets, or that supply local craftspeople with materials.

Most often, the herb garden is filled with culinary herbs, in which case it should be near the kitchen or vegetable garden. And, of course, herbs can be planted just for their beauty, their scents, and the hum of the bees they attract.

Italian Garden

Italian gardens are architectural, symmetrical, and formal. They feature stone staircases, balustrades, terraces, fountains, cascades, niches, statues, colonnades, large terra-cotta pots, pergolas, and porticoes in concert with a grand axis and villa. Inspired and influenced by ancient Roman gardens, Italian Renaissance gardens blossomed in the fifteenth century. Though ancient Roman gardens had vanished centuries earlier, their stone ruins remained, as did detailed descriptions by such writers as Pliny the Younger. Renaissance gardeners learned and extrapolated from these relics of the past.

Italian Renaissance gardens were a radical departure from the much simpler European gardens that preceded them. The gardens of the Middle Ages were set apart from the house, laid out with four quadrants, enclosed, often featuring a well in the center. Beginning in the fifteenth century, Italian architects linked the garden to the villa, with an axis leading directly from the villa through the garden. Working with the hilly terrain, the designers created terraces joined by flights of stairs. They incorporated distant views, especially on coastal estates. Like the ancient Romans, they were fond of topiaries, pergolas, and hardscape.

Flowers, some brought back from Africa and the western hemisphere, were grown where they could be viewed from the villa. Parterres were made of angles and straight lines until the seventeenth century, when gardeners embraced the French scrolls and curlicues of Le Nôtre. Italian gardens of the Renaissance included orchards and woodlands, usually on the periphery of the main garden. Bay laurel, cypress, firs, and various evergreens grew in the woodland gardens while the *bosco*, or outer ring, was made up of native trees and understory plants. Almonds, apricots, cherries, figs, lemons, oranges, pears, and plums filled the orchards. The tradition of planting fruit trees in a quincunx pattern continued from the Middle Ages.

Shade and water were important elements in the warm and sunny climate of Italy. Thick vines draped pergolas. Trees spread their limbs over seating. Water tinkled and sparkled in fountains and cascades. Pools shimmered.

Italian gardens reached their epitome in the mid-sixteenth century with such gardens as the lavish Villa d'Este at Tivoli, and were influential throughout Europe. Over the years, trees matured into large specimens, relaxing the precision of earlier years. Flowers, though always present in Italian gardens, became less important. Soon, French garden ideas dominated. In the eighteenth century, the landscape movement swept away many formal Italian gardens, especially those outside Italy.

Yet, Italian gardens endured. In 1892, the artist and landscape designer Charles A. Platt published his photo book *Italian Gardens* after a visit with his brother to Italy's remaining Renaissance gardens. A few years later, Edith Wharton went to Italy to study old Italian gardens, many nearly gone or dilapidated. She praised the genius of their designs and described and analyzed them in her masterful bestseller, *Italian Villas and Their Gardens*. The book, with illustrations by Maxfield Parrish, was published in 1904. Platt's and Wharton's books and magazine articles ignited a craze for Italian gardens in the United States. Estate owners added them to their properties or transformed their entire estates into Italian gardens.

Italianate gardens are widely recognized for their strong bones and the sense of calm and repose they offer the visitor.

Today, Italianate gardens are widely recognized for their strong bones and the sense of calm and repose they offer the visitor. Meant for a Mediterranean climate, they work best in similar climes, but elements such as pergolas and stone stairs are at home in any landscape, even one more modest and less formal than a classic Italian garden.

Japanese Garden

Japanese gardens, oases of tranquility composed of raked sand, boulders, moss, and evergreens, are richly layered with symbolism. Islands, waterfalls, and the essence of Buddha are conveyed via thoughtfully placed stones. A plum blossom connotes rebirth. A tree is a forest. Various elements and their imagery evoke the natural world. Though highly designed, they represent the undesigned. A Japanese garden suggests the wilds of nature to the informed visitor, who sees mountains, rivers, and forests in the tiny courtyard garden, known as a *tsuboniwa*, meant to be viewed from a window.

Japanese gardens grew out of the garden traditions of China and Korea. In the first years of the seventh century, a Korean priest visited the Japanese court, bringing with him books describing the legends of the immortals who dwelled on mystical islands. These were represented by stone groupings in gardens. The first Japanese envoy to China, visiting in 607 CE, was astonished at the Chinese emperor's magnificent pleasure park of islands and lakes which reputedly took a million men to create. He decided to make his own version at home in Japan.

Centuries of garden-making ensued, and the Japanese infused Chinese and Korean design concepts with their own philosophical and emotional meanings. They described nature through artifice. Their gardens were able to convey much more than they could actually contain.

In the Heian period, Japanese gardens were made up of lakes, islands, arched bridges, pavilions, and gravel plazas. The court attendant Murasaki Shikibu described them in great detail in her novel, *The Tale of Genji*, written in the first decade of the eleventh century. An important aspect of her novel is the association of emotions with the garden experience.

Buddhism was introduced into Japan in the eighth century. During the Kamakura and Muromachi periods, Zen Buddhism, a particularly Japanese form of Buddhism, flourished. Gardens became smaller, and more simplified, though many still included ponds, bridges, pavilions, and waterfalls. Gardens made only of rocks, gravel, and sand began to appear. This was called a *karesansui* or dry garden. It was during this period that *Sakuteiki,* the first known Japanese gardening manual, was written—perhaps the world's first book devoted to garden design. The author, Tachibana no Toshitsuna, advised, "Visualize the famous landscapes of our country and come to understand their most interesting points. Re-create the essence of those scenes in the garden but do so interpretatively, not strictly."

Tea gardens, though already present, reached perfection in the following years, during the Azuchi-Momoyama period. Here, guests would be welcomed for the highly ritualized tea ceremony. In addition to stones, sand, and moss, a tea garden included a *chashitsu* (tea house), stone basin, and perhaps a stone lantern or gate. Within the tea house, the ceremony was conducted with treasured items such as handmade ceramic tea bowls and vases, specially arranged flowers, and an iron kettle.

During the first half of the seventeenth century, the Japanese grew angry at the missionaries who had come to their land, fearing they were bringing European dominance. In response, they banished nearly all foreigners and forbade international travel, secluding Japan from the rest of the world for the next 241 years. During these years of isolation, the Edo period, Japan missed the industrial and scientific advances being made elsewhere but enjoyed peace. Art and culture flourished.

The notion of grandeur was reintroduced and with it, large stroll gardens. Stroll gardens, with their winding paths, central ponds, and sights, took some of their inspiration from woodblock prints. In an era when even nobility could not travel, stroll gardens offered the pleasure and illusion of a journey. A stroll was an excursion through a series of artfully contrived scenes. Some garden historians believe stroll gardens influenced the gardens of the English landscape movement.

In the mid-nineteenth century, Commodore Perry, arriving with four ships, forcibly "opened" Japan to trade with the United States. Russian, British, French, and Dutch navies followed suit. An unexpected outcome of these incursions was that the West was exposed to Japanese gardens and the wonderous variety of plants that flourished on the islands. Less than a decade later, plants collected in Japan were propagated and sold by Parsons Nursery in Long Island. Japanese-style gardens began to appear in the West.

Japanese gardens are infused with the spirituality of Shintoism, Confucianism, Taoism, and Buddhism. They offer respite and serenity. Unlike Western gardens, they do not offer a colorful succession of horticultural changes through the year. Instead, it is the seasons themselves that lend quiet drama. Highly stylized, Japanese gardens are instructive of what can be achieved in a small space. They can inform an entire landscape or be one of several gardens within a landscape.

Kitchen Garden, Potager

The first gardens were for growing food. Gardens of worship, pleasure, and repose evolved out of the earliest food gardens as gardeners realized that their grape arbors offered refreshing shade for sitting, and that gardens could be pleasant to look at. Household gardens for food—kitchen gardens, which might include flowers and a place to sit—have been with us as long as we have been gardening.

In his 1633 book, *New England's Prospect*, William Wood describes seeing fields of corn and hay and "pleasant gardens with kitchen gardens," telling his readers that "whatever grows in England, grows as well [in the New England colonies], many things being better and larger." He goes on to list turnips, parsnips, carrots, radishes, muskmelons, pumpkins, cucumbers, onions, and many herbs. The beds in colonial kitchen gardens were often raised, and laid out geometrically with paths, as the gardens of Europe had been laid out for centuries. Herbs, vegetables, and flowers were mixed together.

Native Americans had been growing fields of corn, beans, pumpkins, squash, gourds, tobacco, and sunflowers long before the English arrived. In fact, they had hybridized corn for so long that it is impossible to know what the original plant was like. They planted pumpkins and squash among the corn and bean hills, so that the corn stalks gave support to the vines. Interestingly, when the English arrived, watermelons (native to Africa) were grown throughout North America, west to the Rockies. It is believed that Spaniards, who arrived in the New World prior to the English, brought watermelon seeds with them.

The colonists learned from the horticulturally skilled native inhabitants, but also brought generations of garden customs and knowledge with them, which they adapted to their new land.

The great seventeenth- and eighteenth-century estates of England grew fruits and vegetables in walled kitchen gardens of many acres. These vast, enclosed spaces included paths, beds, hot houses, cold frames, arbors, and outbuildings.

They required large staffs of skilled and unskilled gardeners to maintain. Originally situated close to the house, they were eventually moved away and out of sight. These walled kitchen gardens, with sun-warmed microclimates near the walls themselves, provided fruit, vegetables, and flowers for the lord of the manor and his family to consume and sell. Laborers kept their own small plots at their homes outside the walled garden, but might also receive a portion of the produce they worked so hard to cultivate.

Whether in large gardens or small, vegetables were grown using raised beds or squares until American reformers in the mid-nineteenth century argued that it would be more efficient to grow garden crops in the same manner as field crops, such as corn. They advocated planting in long, straight rows with the aid of horse-drawn plows, hoes, and cultivators. No more old-fashioned, cumbersome square beds and cross-paths! A horse and plow require ten to twelve feet to turn at the end of a row, so it took the horseless wheel hoe to make the mechanical cultivation of rows possible and popular in small gardens.

A garden that is plowed every year is not conducive to perennials, so flowers were moved into their own gardens, apart from the vegetables. At the same time, patent medicines replaced home herbal remedies so housewives stopped growing herbs in their home gardens. Lastly, barbed wire kept livestock in their pastures, making it no longer necessary to enclose the garden. Thus, we have the large, rectangular vegetable garden planted with row upon straight row of cabbages, tomatoes, cucumbers, lettuces, beets, broccoli, cauliflower, melons, and string beans, and plowed under before planting each year.

Not everyone embraced the garden row. Some preferred the slow pleasure of a hand hoe and the joys of mingling flowers and vegetables. But by the twentieth century, rows were the prevalent way of growing vegetables—except by Italian immigrants. Between 1880 and 1924, four million Italians arrived in America, settling primarily in cities, where they maintained the old ways of gardening in squares and raised beds.

Interest in vegetable gardening waned with the rise of the automobile (and falloff of available manure). Trucks and trains transported commercially produced fruits, vegetables, dairy products,

and meats to grocery stores, so why grow one's own? World War I, with the threat of inflated food prices and shortages, and later the Great Depression, temporarily renewed interest. World War II brought the Victory Garden and the notion that it was patriotic to grow your own vegetables. The suburban boom that followed World War II included backyard vegetable gardens with rows of tomatoes, peppers, cucumbers, and other vegetables, though the convenience of grocery stores remained paramount. Interest was again renewed with the back-to-the-land movement of the 1970s.

In the latter quarter of the twentieth century, writer and garden designer Rosemary Verey, inspired by the writings of William Lawson, decided to take out the "utilitarian rows" of vegetables in her gardens at Barnsley House, and create a potager. Popular in France, where rows never quite caught on, potagers are ornamental vegetable gardens planted in beds and parterres. One of the most famous potagers is the Chateau de Villandry, in the Loire Valley of France. Verey made paths from bricks she rescued from demolished buildings, installed arbors and trellises, and planted a rich assortment of vegetables and flowers. She wrote about her potager in her book *Making of a Garden,* designed potagers for others, and welcomed visitors and photographers, inspiring gardeners on both sides of the Atlantic to turn their plain vegetable gardens into something similar.

Formal potagers, old-time kitchen gardens, no-frills rototilled vegetable gardens with rows, and informal cottage gardens coexist in today's landscape. They might include espaliered and dwarf fruit trees, vines, and berries, as well as herbs, perennials, and annuals—plus, the main attraction, an abundance of vegetables for the table.

> The beds in colonial kitchen gardens were often raised, and laid out geometrically with paths, as the gardens of Europe had been.

Labyrinth, Maze

The words "labyrinth" and "maze" both refer to a design of pathways and are commonly used interchangeably. In fact, there is a difference between the two. A labyrinth is unicursal, that is, there is one path. The entrance opening and exit opening are one and the same. You enter, follow the non-branching path to the center or goal, and continue on the path to the exit. The classic labyrinth design has seven rings, but rings can be added four at a time, making eleven, fifteen, and more, while maintaining the integrity of the design. The path is not a spiral. Early seven-ring labyrinths were carved into stone, impressed in tiles, imprinted on coins, written as graffiti, or laid out in the landscape in widely divergent areas of the world for thousands of years. There are many variations beyond the classic labyrinth, but they are all unicursal.

A maze is multicursal, meaning it has branching paths and dead ends, it can have more than one exit or entrance. A maze is entertainment, a puzzle to be solved.

Labyrinths, with their single path, are often perceived as spiritual, a way to focus the mind. Walking a labyrinth has been used for meditation, penance, an act of pilgrimage, ritual, sacred practice, and for grieving. Over 500 stone labyrinths remain in Scandinavia, notably the Tralleborg labyrinth on an island in Sweden, now part of a national park. There are numerous ancient turf labyrinths in England and Germany such as the Dalby labyrinth in Yorkshire, England, thought to be one of the oldest.

Historians are not certain when labyrinths were first made of evergreen hedges, but by the Renaissance, they had become high-prestige garden elements in the landscapes of royalty. These were permanent features, requiring a heavy investment in labor and time. It took five to ten years for a hedge to grow to maturity and once mature, maintenance entailed precise clipping. Gardeners developed new and intricate layouts: square, rectangular, trapezoidal, octagonal. Soon they added surprise and confusion by creating hedged puzzle mazes with multiple or dead-end paths as a challenging entertainment for the guests who entered. The pathways might be decorated with benches and fountains. Ambitious gardeners made mazes that included grottoes, tunnels, and bridges. Several mazes were sometimes connected.

A labyrinth is unicursal, that is, there is one path. A maze is multicursal, meaning it has branching paths and dead ends.

The hedge maze at Hampton Court, the oldest in the UK, covers a third of an acre. Made originally of hornbeam for William III of Orange in the late seventeenth century, the hedges were later replanted with yew. The maze attracts visitors from all over the globe and has spawned imitations on a smaller scale.

In addition to providing amusement for perambulating visitors, hedge mazes were meant to be enjoyed from second- and third-story castle windows, much the way parterres were enjoyed. Ancient, new, and restored hedge mazes attract many visitors today. The added dimension of aerial photography enhances the experience.

For the home landscape, church and hospital gardens, and public parks and schools, many gardeners embrace the simple stone, shell, or raised turf labyrinth. This is essentially a pattern on the ground. Labyrinths can be made in a small space, ten or eleven feet across, tucked at the edge of a forest, or incorporated in a courtyard or healing garden. Paths are made of gravel, bark mulch, paving, or grass. The goal or center might be a stone plinth, boulder, or gravel circle. Even the smallest labyrinth of this type can take fifteen minutes or so to navigate (if you do not cheat and step out of the path), thus slowing the mind. Indeed, labyrinths have become such widespread garden features, commercial suppliers now sell preprinted weed-blocking landscape fabric, making installation nearly foolproof.

Let's Get Lost

Both labyrinths and mazes have enjoyed renewed and increased popularity since the 1980s. While traditional hedge mazes retain their trendy status in formal gardens, corn and sunflower mazes have become the stars of agritourism. By the end of the summer and into the autumn, corn and sunflowers soar eight or more feet in the air blocking views beyond the immediate path. These mazes vary in difficulty from simple enough for small children and comfortably navigable, to so difficult that visitors are given an emergency cell phone number to call if they can't find their way out. After dark, flashlight tours are frequently offered during the week leading up to Halloween. Corn and sunflower mazes cover from a few to as many as thirty acres. The designs usually change each year and are themed, requiring considerable skill on the part of the farmer-designer. Some mazes have clues at stopping places interspersed throughout, or signs featuring trivia about the maze theme. There are viewing towers and even balloon rides that take visitors over the maze.

Landscape Gardening

Landscape gardening sprang from the work of William Kent in the eighteenth century and expanded and flourished under Capability Brown. Prior to Kent, there was a growing interest in incorporating a more natural informality into gardens. Some English gardeners left trees unclipped. They planted trees and shrubs in irregular patterns rather than rows, taking a few steps away from formality.

Kent, as Horace Walpole famously wrote, "leaped the fence, and saw all nature was a garden." Inspired by nature and painting, Kent created gardens that were idealized landscapes. He eschewed the straight lines and right angles that had ruled gardens in previous centuries, and replaced them with curves. His pictur-esque landscapes reflected poetry and art, with subtle references to Greek and Latin literature that knowledgeable visitors would understand and appreciate.

Brown was less interested in literary references, though he included allusions such as temples in the views he created in his landscapes. He called his work "place making" and carefully orchestrated the placement of trees in sweep-ing lawns. He sculpted gently rolling hills and turned streams into serpentine lakes over which he built arched bridges. Ha-has were built to keep livestock and deer from coming close to the manor. There were curving drives for carriages to transport guests from outlook to outlook, and paths for walking.

Humphrey Repton coined the phrase "landscape garden."

Brown's romanticized landscapes required considerable intervention to achieve. He erased all existing formal elements. He swept away ter-races, flower gardens, parterres, and former gardens. He banished the kitchen garden from proximity to the house (and kitchen), moving it well out of sight. If workers' cottages were in view, or entire villages, those also went. For this,

he faced some criticism in his day, but his work was also widely imitated and influential.

Humphrey Repton coined the phrase "landscape garden." He built upon Brown's work, while humanizing it. He reinstituted flower beds, gravel paths, and terraces close to the house. His gardens were convenient and comfortable in the domestic sphere, while ensconced in the beautiful artifice of a perfected landscape.

In the nineteenth century, Frederick Law Olmsted took the best aspects of the landscape movement and incorporated them into his parks, notably Central Park in New York City, which he designed with Calvert Vaux. The urban park movements in the United States and UK also drew heavily on the ideas of landscape gardening.

Many elements of landscape gardening endure today, though not on the grand scale of Brown, nor with complete fidelity. We do not knock down villages that spoil our view. Yet, a winding path through parklike grounds continues to hold appeal.

The underlying philosophy of landscape gardening continues to influence public and private design. It is evident on college campuses. We see the influence of landscape gardening in the vast acres of our public parks. We see the influence in deep American backyards with swards of grass and clumps of large shade trees.

Lawn

There is little mention of lawns in early writings, nor depictions in art. The Middle Ages saw flowery meads, which included grasses and flowers. Chamomile and clover lawns were also grown during the Middle Ages.

André Le Nôtre installed a *tapis vert* (green carpet) at Versailles in the eighteenth century. The landscape movement in England emphasized large sweeps of turf—greenswards, as the Romantics called them—kept short by cutting with scythes, or grazing sheep. Capability Brown, a leader of the movement, demolished stone terraces and gravel forecourts and replaced them with grass. The climate, especially in England, was ideal for growing lawns. In 1830, Edwin Budding invented the lawn mower and alleviated the challenging work of scything. Anyone could have a lawn.

Finding only annual grasses that were quickly depleted by livestock, seventeenth-century American colonists on the Atlantic coast imported perennial grass seed for their hayfields and pastures (along with weeds such as plantain, known to Native Americans as "Englishman's foot" because everywhere the English walked, plantain appeared!). The climate in the colonies, with frigid winters and hot, humid summers, was not ideal for grass. Nevertheless, the imported seeds naturalized and spread. In 1780, the Shakers began commercially producing seed for pastures.

The narrow area between a typical house and road of the era was not grass but herbs and flowers, or beaten earth, until George Washington (inspired by European fashions) installed a bowling green and deer park at Mount Vernon. Thomas Jefferson, also taken with European garden trends, grew large expanses of grass at Monticello. As printed images of these estates appeared in newspapers and on postcards, wealthy Americans began to plant lawns at their own residences.

After the Civil War, the public park movement, led by Frederick Law Olmstead, inspired the first planned communities and suburbs. Houses were set back thirty feet from the road, which was lined with shade trees. Affluent homeowners planted front lawns that blended from one property to the next without the impediment of fences or hedges, making the entire neighborhood feel parklike.

Returning from service in the Union Army, Orlando McLean Scott began producing and selling buggies and weed-free grass seed, which he marketed to farmers. In 1907, his son Dwight suggested that they start a mail order business to sell grass seed for lawns. The business prospered and grew.

At the same time, inventors were busy inventing tools to make lawn care easier. Amariah Hills of Hockanum (now East Hartford), Connecticut, obtained the first U.S. patent for a reel lawn mower in 1868 and founded the Archimedean Lawn Mower Company. In 1871, Joseph Lessler of Buffalo, New York, received a patent for his lawn sprinkler, which attached to a hose. Flexible hoses have been in use since ancient Greek times, when they were made of intestines. Later hoses were made of canvas or stitched leather and found their way into horticulture.

In 1830, Edwin Budding invented the lawn mower and alleviated the challenging work of scything.

Rubber magnate B.F. Goodrich of Akron, Ohio, made the garden hose ubiquitous. First available to firefighters in the 1870s, Goodrich's rubber hose quickly became indispensable for lawn and garden care.

In the 1920s, the rise of the automobile and affordable train travel led to more suburbs, as workers moved out from the densely populated, smoky cities to surrounding leafy neighborhoods that were being built. An even greater wave of suburb expansion followed World War II, spurred by the ready availability of loans to returning soldiers and the explosion of mass-produced housing. Newly built post-WWII tract houses were for ordinary Americans, not just the wealthy, but like the earlier suburban properties, a key feature was the front lawn.

The front lawn was, and still is, the public face of a property. Family life generally takes place in the backyard. Here, too, there is usually a lawn which the residents use for recreation. But it is the front lawn that makes a statement. Its upkeep is often seen as a civic duty to the community. Dandelions in one lawn soon spread to all the surrounding lawns.

Lawn care is a mega-billion-dollar industry in the United States. Today, one can choose between a standard push mower, riding gasoline-engine lawn mower, robot mower, electric mower, or a solar-battery-powered mower. For those who do not want to take care of the lawn themselves, there are many lawn care companies eager to take on the task for a fee.

In recent years, an increasing number of homeowners have begun to question the sustainability of maintaining a perfect, weed-free lawn, but grass remains the most-grown "crop" in America, with considerable resources spent on its maintenance. Moles, voles, and chipmunks tunnel beneath our lawns; cutworms and grubs eat the roots of the grass; dandelions, plantains, and other weeds intrude; and an abundance of water is required to keep the grass green. A perfect lawn requires hard work and is a coveted status symbol. It is a pleasant contrast to borders, shrubs, and trees, and is a pleasure to walk or play on. A lawn makes an attractive floor for the garden. The ideal of a smooth, velvety green carpet with perfect mowing stripes prevails.

Seed companies offer blends for specific site conditions such as sun, shade, or acidic soils. However, with concerns about water usage, herbicides, pesticides, and the environment, there is a growing movement away from a monoculture lawn to a mixed or yeoman's lawn and clover lawns. Mixed and clover lawns require less water, fertilizer, and mowing than a lawn of all fine grasses. There is also a movement toward the reduction or elimination of lawns, replacing them with shrubs, flowers, ornamental grasses, paths, and vegetables. Nevertheless, lawns are an icon of the good life. Most gardeners want at least a small patch of grass where children can run barefoot. Homeowners with little interest in gardens often want only grass.

Lighting, Lantern

As long as people have been lighting the interiors of their homes, they have carried lanterns into their gardens at night. Egyptian, Greek, and Roman terra-cotta lanterns burned olive or nut oil, or sometimes beeswax, casting only a small circle of light.

Lighting offers safety on paths and stairs. It can enhance the ambience of a garden in the evening, casting mysterious shadows or bringing attention to a specific feature.

For thousands of years, the night garden has been associated with imagination and poetry, moonlight and stars. Fireflies, found in the eastern half of the United States, in Asia, and in Central and South America, twinkle magically in the dark garden and meadow, delighting children. Japanese gardeners, though they deeply appreciated these gifts of illumination from nature, imported Chinese bronze and stone lanterns from Korea in the sixth century. By the sixteenth century, they were an important component of Japanese gardens and the tea ceremony. Japanese stone lanterns, and concrete reproductions, are iconic garden ornaments throughout the world today. Traditionally fueled by the pith of the yellow-flowered shrub Japanese kerria, such lanterns now burn candles or oil, or simply decorate the garden.

Japanese stone lanterns, and concrete reproductions, are iconic garden ornaments throughout the world today.

In 1820, Paris started using gas lamps to illuminate its streets. In September 1882, Thomas Edison turned on 3000 incandescent bulbs on Pearl Street in New York City. Soon after, he developed the electric meter and began commercially producing electric light fixtures, forever changing the way we live.

The porch or front door light, and often a lamppost at the end of a driveway, moved electric light into domestic outdoor spaces. In 1952, John Watson of Texas opened John Watson Landscape Illumination, offering his services to wealthy clients, hotels, and museums. Landscape lighting design had become a profession.

Lighting is used to transform a tree into a nighttime focal point, wash a patio in light, draw guests out into the garden, or line a deck railing. There are lights that are directed down, and those that are trained up; lights set in wells in the ground; underwater lights for the pool. We can play with and control shadows. Fixtures are made of ceramic; metals such as brass, steel, or aluminum; and plastics in various styles. It is crucial that fixtures look as good during the day when they are off as at night when they are turned on. It is also important that they be placed to not interfere with maintenance tasks such as lawn mowing or snow shoveling.

With low-voltage and LED lights, outdoor lighting is more affordable than the early days. Outdoor solar lighting makes it not only possible, but easy, to bring light into the garden, as it doesn't require digging trenches and running wires. Solar lanterns store energy from the sun during the day and turn automatically on when darkness comes. They can be set for motion activation. Some flicker to look like a candle. Others are bright enough to illuminate a walk or entranceway.

Lighting can also pollute the night sky, so that the stars appear faint, many invisible. In much of the United States, you cannot see the Milky Way. Night lighting disrupts the life cycles and behavior of plants and animals. Even insects are affected. Lighting a few candles or lanterns on occasion is benign, but flood-lights and outdoor electric lights left on all night are not. Of course, home gardeners are not the main source of light pollution, but neither do we want to contribute to it.

A thoughtfully lit garden can add hours of enjoyment. Some gardeners, especially those who work long days or dislike heat, garden at night, with a battery-operated headlamp. Yet, as the gardeners of old China understood, nothing is quite as moving as a garden bathed only in the light of a full moon.

Meadow

A meadow is a field of grasses dotted with wildflowers, traditionally cut for hay. Today, ecologists and gardeners cultivate meadows as a substitute for lawns, as a way to attract wildlife, encourage biodiversity, and conserve water. A meadow with grasses and wildflowers gently swaying in the breeze is also beautiful. Such spaces can include vast acreage, such as the eighty-six-acre meadow at Longwood Gardens in Pennsylvania, or take up only a small area, such as the front yard of a residential property.

In the 1990s, with the rising green movement, there was increased interest in creating meadow gardens—so much so that colorful tins of "shake and grow" wildflower seeds were widely advertised and offered in gift shops and catalogs. Gardeners quickly discovered that creating an attractive meadow takes considerably more skill and work than just a quick flip of the wrist. Effective methods for planting and maintaining meadows were developed.

There was also a growing interest in restoring lost prairie lands in the private landscape. At one time, prairies—tall grass, short grass, and mixed grass—covered most of central North America. Agriculture, construction, alien species, and fire suppression have destroyed from half to nearly all of the prairie lands in the states between the Rocky Mountains and Lake Michigan.

Meadows are planted with sun-loving native grasses and wildflowers, or a mix of natives and compatible perennials that have naturalized. A few perennials for meadows include black-eyed Susans, butterfly weed, daisies, purple coneflowers, queen of the prairie, and annual sunflowers. Bulbs can also be added for spring interest.

Although considered low maintenance, meadows can be vulnerable to weeds. Common nettles can quickly dominate an entire meadow. Oriental bittersweet sends its long orange roots great distances underground. It is essential that the entire plot be thoroughly cleared of all vegetation and seeds before planting the meadow, but even with this effort, unwanted weeds arrive. Meadows are cut once or twice a year to prevent trees and shrubs from taking hold.

Simple mown paths through a meadow encourage visitors to stroll among the grasses and flowers, watch the butterflies and bees up close, and explore. It is nice, too, to have a place in a meadow to watch the changes wrought by the seasons, the flash of a summer storm, or the flight of a bird overhead.

Memorial Garden

Rural or garden cemeteries, such as Mount Auburn in Cambridge, Massachusetts, and Laurel Hill in Philadelphia, were created to be places for the living as much as for the dead. With rolling lawns, ponds, shade trees, shrubs, hedges, fences, broad walkways, and artistic monuments to the deceased, these spaces were designed as inviting sanctuaries for the working class and wealthy alike. Families could stroll, picnic, enjoy the scenery, and escape the soot and noise of the city, while also remembering their lost loved ones.

The forerunner of garden cemeteries was the New Haven Burying Ground in New Haven, Connecticut, created in 1796. Until then, cemeteries were in church yards where the dead were buried close together and on top of each other as the yards ran out of space. They were mournful places. New Haven Burying Ground was the first municipal solution to this problem in the United States.

Mount Auburn Cemetery, which notably adopted the euphemistic word "cemetery" from the Greek for "resting place," rather than burial ground, was designed by Henry Alexander Scammell Dearborn, the first president of the Massachusetts Horticultural Society. It was originally seventy-two acres and later expanded to 175 acres straddling Cambridge and Watertown. Dearborn was influenced by the English landscape gardening movement and Père Lachaise Cemetery in Paris. Mount Auburn inspired the rural cemetery (or garden cemetery) movement.

The Sunken Garden at Princess Diana's former home at Kensington Palace was transformed into a formal memorial garden . . . in her honor.

Rural cemeteries soon appeared in Maine, New York, Connecticut, Wisconsin, Pennsylvania, and elsewhere. Here, families enjoyed fresh air and tranquility on their days off. By the end of the nineteenth century, however, hundreds of landscaped public parks gained precedence as the place for families to escape the pressures of urban life. Notions of death and burial changed. In response, new cemeteries were more sterile, with gravestones lined up in rows. Cremation was often preferred to burial.

A recent movement is the creation of memorial or remembrance gardens to commemorate the loss of a loved one. This can be a private garden incorporated into one's own landscape, or a public garden of remembrance. Sometimes it is as simple as a tree with a plaque. We see roadside wooden crosses painted white and encircled with a ring of flowers at the site of fatal car accidents along highways and backroads. The Sunken Garden at Princess Diana's former home at Kensington Palace was transformed into a formal memorial garden by replanting it as a white garden in her honor. The garden writer and wine expert Hugh Johnson planted an acre his father had leased out for grazing livestock in Kent, England, as a memorial garden after his father's death.

Home memorial gardens often include favorite or symbolic plants, a bench, or perhaps a paved area. They can be an excuse to purchase a piece of art or a lead urn. Often there is a stone with an inscription, such as a line of poetry.

Backyard remembrance gardens are also made for beloved pets. This might be a flat fieldstone from the property set in a bed of ground cover, or, more elaborately, a concrete or metal statue of a cat or dog with flowers and a bench.

Happily, there is renewed interest in the rural or garden cemeteries made in the nineteenth century, with their horticultural and historical value now widely recognized. Some have sought status as arboretums. Mount Auburn is listed by the National Trust. Many of these places welcome the public for concerts, yoga, weddings, and other activities. Beautifully mature gardens as much as graveyards, their futures seem ensured.

A memorial garden incorporated into a home garden, however, is likely to be ephemeral. The next resident might find it disturbing or not to his or her taste. One is planting it for oneself and the survivors, not necessarily for the ages. A remembrance garden that is beautiful and comforting with subtle or universal symbols of the beloved has greater chance of longevity, but even if the garden is fleeting, as is life itself, it serves its purpose in the present.

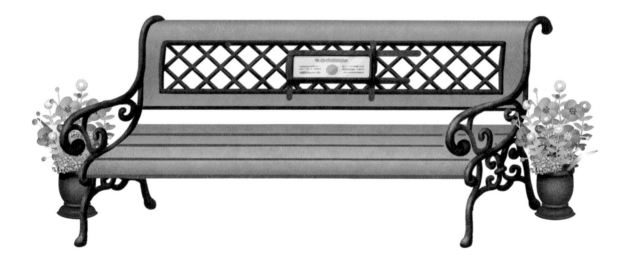

Orchard

An orchard is a plot of land dedicated to growing fruit trees. It can cover vast acreage or a corner of a home garden. It can be devoted to one kind of fruit, or contain a mix. Nuts (which are also fruits) are grown in orchards, as are olives, though often these are called groves. A grove is a group of trees with little or no undergrowth, so an orchard is a grove, but a grove, which can include any kind of tree, is not necessarily an orchard. A group of mixed nut trees may also be called a nuttery.

The trees in an informal orchard might be planted in a random pattern, but traditionally, especially where productivity is a concern, trees are planted in rows, squares, a quincunx, or other pattern to facilitate pollination and harvesting. Ancient Egyptians planted their mixed orchards of date, fig, and olive trees in a quincunx or rows of sunken planting holes with mud walls up to two feet high. Their orchards included a well or irrigation pool filled with water from the Nile. Men and boys climbed the trees to pick the fruits, which they dropped into ceramic jars, baskets, or nets. By the New Kingdom (1550 BCE to 1077 BCE), tomb illustrations show formal walled orchards.

Alexander the Great brought dwarf apple trees—called by historian Theophrastus the spring apple, later known as the paradise apple—to Greece from his expeditions in Asia Minor, introducing dwarf fruit trees to Europe. Self-rooting, the dwarf apple was eagerly adopted and improved by the Romans, who were skilled at grafting and pruning. They grew both standard and dwarf trees.

Romans introduced the apple for eating and cider to Britain and other northern Europeans. Peasant families in the Dark Ages kept a couple of fruit trees if they could, but it was the monastic communities that preserved the Roman horticultural skills. They kept orchards of apple, pear, and walnut trees. By the seventeenth century, writers such as John Tradescant and John Evelyn were offering advice on grafting, pruning, and propagating fruit trees, as well as their opinions on the best aspect for an orchard.

American colonists made orchards from their own seedlings and did not bother to graft or prune in the early years. Their orchards were primarily apple trees, for the prodigious amounts of cider they produced. From 1820 to 1870, there was a mild mania for pears in New England. By then, grafting and pruning were widely practiced.

Orchards are best sited in sunny locations free of frost pockets and strong winds. Birds, insects, deer, and mice love the sweetness of fruit as much as we do, so nets, cages, shiny strips of acetate, inward-slanting deer fences, and other repellants are employed to keep them at bay.

Fruit trees are pruned annually for the most abundant fruiting. When space is at a premium in a small home garden, or when a farmer desires the maximum amount of fruit per acre, trees can be pruned into espaliers, fans, or cordons and grown on wires in rows in the orchard. This increases the amount of fruit from each tree, while greatly reducing the footprint. It is labor intensive in the first formative years.

Orchards are generally underplanted with grass and clover, which are mown but allowed to grow longer than a lawn. Bulbs also work well in the orchard and can be left to naturalize and spread. The orchard at Chanticleer, the early twentieth-century estate garden outside Philadelphia, is underplanted with tens of thousands of white daffodils. An orchard in spring, with fruit blossoms and bulbs in bloom, is a thing of great beauty. Indeed, orchards have attracted many artists over the years, including Claude Monet, Vincent Van Gogh, and Alfred Sisley.

In addition to providing fruit for the table, orchards offer a delightful spot for entertaining. Going back thousands of years, farmers have held harvest festivals in their orchards and enjoyed the shade of their fruit trees. Today, orchards are a favorite setting for farm-to-table events. Home orchardists, too, can set a pretty table and a few chairs under an apple tree, light a lantern, and invite friends into the orchard for dinner.

Trees are planted in rows, squares, a quincunx, or another pattern to facilitate pollination and harvesting.

Ornament

Ornaments give a garden individuality. They express the gardener's personality. Ornaments can change to reflect the season, appear at the whim of the gardener, or lend permanence to a space dominated by the impermanence of plants. "Ornament," garden historian George Plumptre tells us, "has elevated the garden from being a place of production to a place of pleasure."

The urge to decorate predates written history. Potters scratched horizontal bands and crosshatches into the damp clay of their pots. Our ancestors drew pictures on cave walls and drilled holes in seashells to string them for necklaces. That urge exists in us still. We collect vintage watering cans and arrange them on a silvered picnic table near the zinnias. We spend a fortune on a mossy stone cherub to rest by the reflecting pool. We amuse ourselves with a whirligig by the front door or a gnome in the pansies.

The venerable formal gardens of the past relied on long-lasting pieces like statuary, urns, sundials, and obelisks made of stone or lead for their ornaments. These salutary works of art reflected the owner's learning, taste, and status. We admire them still. They draw the eye and create an atmosphere of tranquility and antiquity.

Whatever the ornaments, they should complement the style of the garden.

But decoration need not be so august. The idea of bottle trees—colored bottles placed on the ends of leafless tree branches—came to the American South with slaves from the African kingdom of Kongo. Originally considered southern garden folk art, bottle trees are now so mainstream that you can purchase a metal "tree" for your bottles or even an entire premade tree, no matter where you live.

For kitsch, nothing rivals the pink plastic flamingo, designed in 1957 by Don Featherstone. An icon of pop culture, the much-maligned lawn ornament was adopted as the official bird of Madison, Wisconsin, in 2009. Nevertheless, more than a few upscale home associations fine homeowners who dare to install a plastic flamingo on their property.

Time for Reflection

Gazing balls, also called garden globes or reflecting balls, are made of mirrored glass, sometimes stainless steel, and set in the garden on a ceramic or concrete pedestal or iron stand. The balls are silver, red, green, blue, or purple. They descend from the mouth-blown glass balls of thirteenth-century Venice, which were favored by kings and nobles. Gazing balls on pedestals were so popular with Victorian gardeners that they often had more than one. Gazing balls charmed American gardeners of the 1930s through the 1950s. Today, mass-produced gazing balls are available at garden centers everywhere. We also see sleek modernist adaptations in contemporary designs.

Vintage and found items are the preferred decorations of many gardeners, from rusted farm equipment overflowing with flowers, to hand-painted signs, antique milk cans, and old tools such as shovels and rakes used as yard decor.

Whatever the ornaments, they should complement the style of the garden. Artfully clustered together, they make a statement. Generally, one should see only one ornament or grouping at a time, or a major and lesser ornament and grouping. Ornaments sprinkled sporadically around the garden can confuse the sightline. Placement should make sense to the viewer and add to the narrative of the garden.

Parterre, Knot Garden

A parterre is a formal garden made of enclosed beds separated by paths, in which the overall pattern is the point of the garden. Parterres evolved from Tudor-era knot gardens, which grew out of beds edged with wattle, boards, bones, tiles, or clipped herbs. In time (we first see knots used in 1494), enterprising gardeners planted and shaped the clipped edging to look like interlacing threads or ropes crossed over and under each other. Knot gardens appealed to the Tudors' love of order and symmetry. The knots became the garden itself, no longer mere edging. Interior spaces were planted with flowers, or, in France, vegetables. They were also left as bare earth, or mulched with coal dust, sand, or chalk. The word *parterre* reached England in 1639 from France. It was first used to describe Italian knot gardens. Claude Mollett, of the Mollett dynasty of French nurseryman and gardeners, is credited with developing the parterre in France. André Le Nôtre brought the form to a majestic new level at Versailles, where he created sophisticated parterres covering many acres.

At their height, parterres throughout Europe depicted curlicues, fleurs de lis, coats of arms, and other complex designs planted in clipped box. They were best enjoyed when looked upon from above, often seen from upper windows.

Knot gardens and parterres were a perfect frame for the bedding-out craze that entered the horticultural lexicon in Victorian England. Spaces inside the knots were planted with brightly colored annuals or covered with stones or shells or even colored gravel.

Eventually, first in Europe and later in the United States, knot gardens and parterres became unfashionable. The formality no longer fit with prevailing tastes and it was difficult to support such a labor-intensive undertaking. Many were torn up or left unshorn.

An interest in garden history and restoration has brought knot gardens and parterres back into the landscape. We see them in formal settings maintained by professionals. There are books of patterns. Those reminiscent of Tudor-era gardens of the Middle Ages are prevalent in herb gardens.

Parterres evolved from Tudor-era knot gardens, which grew out of beds edged with wattle, boards, bones, tiles, or clipped herbs.

Path 🦋

Humans made paths before they made gardens. They followed trails left by animals, made trails themselves by repeatedly walking along the same routes, and eventually purposely forged them. Sometimes these paths were shared with other species. Today, it is not uncommon to see a neighborhood cat or wild rabbit using a garden path.

There are three types of garden paths: destination paths, stroll paths, and viewing paths. A destination path is direct, a route from one point to another, such as a walkway from the street to the front door, or an axis in a formal garden. A destination path can be utilitarian, or as with an axis, it can define and organize the garden. A stroll path encourages visitors to move at a leisurely pace around the garden, in conversation or contemplation; there are curves, places to pause, and things to see, such as an urn, arbor, or distant temple. Ancient Chinese, and later Korean and Japanese gardens, featured stroll paths, as did the landscape gardens of eighteenth-century Europe. Viewing paths were constructed so that visitors could look down upon the garden beds. The great gardens of Islam were known for their viewing paths. Each of these types of paths narrates its garden.

There are three types of garden paths: destination paths, stroll paths, and viewing paths.

Except for the gardens of the Far East, paths were made in straight lines until the eighteenth century. The paths of ancient Egypt, Persia, Europe in the Middle Ages, the vast gardens of French nobility, and the formal gardens of Italy were straight. Capability Brown and William Kent introduced meandering paths. Brown thought of them as the garden's itinerary.

In today's gardens, a single path can serve more than one purpose, linking different areas, setting the garden's tone, and informing how it is seen. Paths can be wide enough for two people to walk arm in arm, or for the gardener to push a wheelbarrow.

A challenge in making curved, turned, and meandering paths is that there has to be a reason for the change of direction other than slowing down the walk. It is human nature to take a shortcut. Often, pedestrians wear a foot path across a lawn as a shortcut between intersecting walkways in a park or on a campus. But if shrubs, a tree, or a garden are planted in the bend of a path, the change of direction will make sense, and people will travel along the proscribed path.

Paths can be made of many materials. They can be paved with brick, stone, cement, or tiles. They can be made of beaten earth, gravel, grass, or bark chips. More expensive to install, paved paths offer permanence, low maintenance, and formality. The materials need to blend well with the surrounding architecture of the house and outbuildings. Soft paths such as those made of turf, gravel, or chips made of bark or wood are informal. They are less expensive to install, but wood chips and gravel need refreshing. Grass needs to be cut.

As we walk a garden path, we expect to find pleasure: beautiful flower beds, arbors, blossoming shrubs, heady fragrances, a shimmering pool, or a place to sit. A garden path offers promise.

Patio, Terrace

A patio or terrace is a paved area, usually open to the sky and near or attached to the house, used for outdoor living and leisure activities such as dining, entertaining, sitting, or sunbathing. Though the words are considered synonyms (this is not the kind of terrace that refers to leveled areas of a hillside), we usually use "terrace" when it accompanies a colonial house, and "patio" for more modern architecture such as suburban ranch houses and architecture derived from hot climates.

Patios evolved from Spanish courtyards, which had their origins in Roman courtyards. In America, the first known patio was created in 1565 in St. Augustine, Florida. Patios of swept earth appeared in missions in seventeenth- and eighteenth-century California and New Mexico. On the east coast, African Americans, following the custom of their homelands, also made patios of swept earth. The word terrace is from the Latin *terracea*, which means "earthen," and originally meant a flat area created on a mound of earth.

Today's patio or terrace designer can choose from a variety of artificial and natural paving materials, including concrete pavers in many shapes and sizes, ceramic tiles, granite blocks, bricks, flagstones, and gravel. Concrete pavers make it easy to incorporate curves, multiple levels, steps, built-in benches, pools, and planters, with separate areas for each function. A skilled mason can create any of these things with stone or brick, making a space of singular beauty, especially if the materials are local. However, the expense for both the materials and labor will exceed that of the materials and labor for concrete pavers.

The Levittown Link

After World War II, patios became an essential feature in the American back-yard. With the help of loans from the Department of Veterans Affairs and Federal Housing Administration, and the new availability of affordable, mass-produced housing, such as that built by the Levitt brothers, home ownership in the United States soared.

Most Levittown houses featured sliding glass doors that opened onto a paved patio. Whether they came with the house, or were added later, patios were quickly adopted as an important feature of contemporary living. Mid-twentieth-century patios were usually square or rectangular and made of poured cement slabs or flagstones. A terrace for an antique colonial revival or rustic house would more often be made of flat fieldstones gathered from the property, pea stone, or, more formally, brick or bluestone.

In designing a patio, you need to consider how it will be used, the architecture of the house, and how sunny or shady the site is. A shady site encourages the growth of moss on bricks and stones and is slippery when wet, so gravel or textured concrete would be a better choice. A pergola, tables with umbrellas, or a strategically planted tree can provide shade for the sun-drenched patio. For comfort and ease of movement, there should be at least three feet of space around any planned furniture, such as a chaise or table and chairs.

A terrace or patio is usually placed adjoining the house, often near the kitchen door if the outdoor area is to be used for dining and cooking. However, patios can also be located elsewhere in the garden—such as a second terrace placed where there is a good view of the sunset, or near the vegetable garden as a work area. A well-made and well-thought-out patio or terrace will last several lifetimes, if not longer.

Pergola

A pergola is an ornamental garden structure based on the arbor. It has sturdy uprights made of timber, poles, or masonry and somewhat lighter crossbeams on the top. The sides are open. It is often paved.

In his book, *Houses and Gardens*, Baillie Scott, a leading architect, artist, and garden designer of the Arts and Crafts Movement, wrote that a pergola in a garden is "one of its most attractive features . . . with its paved walk checkered by the shadows of the climbing plants which form its walls and roof."

Pergolas came to England via Italy, where they had adorned gardens since ancient Roman times. Other landscape architects of the era such as Gertrude Jekyll, Edward Lutyens, Harold Peto, and William Robinson were also passionate about pergolas and included them in the gardens they designed. Jekyll devoted an entire chapter to pergolas in her books *Garden Ornaments* and, with Lawrence Weaver, *Gardens for Small Country Houses*. Gustav Stickley, furniture maker and advocate for the American Craftsman style, picked up on the trend. He wrote glowingly of pergolas in his magazine, *The Craftsman*, telling his readers that they connected the house to the garden and provided a pleasurable haven.

Arts and Crafts gardens were designed as an integral part of the house. A pergola might enclose two sides of the garden or overlook a sunken garden. It could hide a drive or it might be attached to the house. Jekyll believed it "should always lead from one definite point to another." She believed something should await at the end of a pergola, such as a summerhouse or an urn. Pergolas served as sheltered passageways in the garden and as pleasant and shady spots for tables and chairs.

Preferred vines for adorning a pergola included clematis, wisteria, Virginia creeper, grape, and honeysuckle. Fruit tree cordons were also grown on pergolas, offering blossoms in spring and fruit at the end of the season. Roses, though often grown on pergolas, were not recommended, as rose flowers face up toward the sun and cannot be enjoyed by those viewing from inside.

Indeed, pergolas were so prevalent in gardens of the period that writers such as Grace Tabor wrote disparagingly of them, railing against "pergola madness!". She believed too many were thoughtlessly placed and served no purpose. She preferred a summerhouse with a roof.

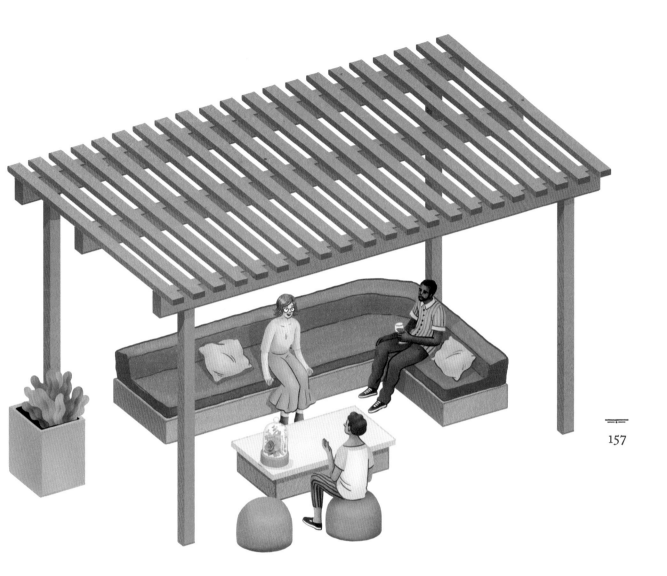

Gardeners today often incorporate pergolas on their decks, creating a dappled retreat. They may be included in gardens, often furnished with a bar or barbecue. A chandelier might hang from the center, or strings of lights might line the crosspieces. They are far less complex and costly than a gazebo, summerhouse, or pavilion, but more substantial than an arbor. In fact, homeowners can purchase prefabricated pergolas made of cedar, redwood, vinyl, or steel. Masons or carpenters offer custom-made pergolas. In areas where the ground freezes, the uprights need to be set on concrete pillars that extend below the frost line. A building permit is often required. It is important to choose a pergola style in keeping with the architecture of the house, especially if the pergola is close to the house. Farther away, a pergola can be more rustic. Wherever it is located, this popular structure can be a romantic yet practical element in a garden and, happily, one of the easiest to add.

Pleach

To pleach is to intertwine one or two rows of trees or shrubs so that they grow into each other and form a wall. It also refers to plaiting an odd number of the same or different species of trunks into a single, braided trunk. Pleaching is used to form decorative stilted hedges, allées, and tunnels, as well as impenetrable barriers. Pleaching was first practiced to form dense living fences and, in flood zones, to form platforms for elevated houses. It became a horticultural art form in seventeenth- and eighteenth-century France, Italy, and England. André Le Nôtre pleached vast lengths of lime and hornbeam in Versailles. Lawrence Johnston was inspired by his visits to France to make a stilt garden at Hidcote Manor, using pleached hornbeams. Vita Sackville-West and Edith Wharton also added pleached lime to their gardens, Sissinghurst and The Mount, respectively, creating appealing, shady walks.

Lime, hornbeam, and plane trees are traditionally used in formal gardens, but modern gardeners are successfully experimenting with a variety of deciduous and evergreen trees. The best trees for pleaching are inosculate: that is, they will self-graft, or, with the encouragement of an abrasion or slit, graft with another species. For instance, linden, beech, and hornbeam trees are inosculate and will grow into each other. Willow is popular because it quickly self-roots and self-grafts.

Trees with straight trunks, all of the same size, are planted in a row and trained on sturdy uprights with bamboo or wire crosspieces. For a stilted hedge, the trunk is kept free of all branches to the desired stilt height. The branches are tied to the crosspieces and eventually intertwined from tree to tree. The branches are clipped and pruned to encourage dense growth and to form a smooth panel. A tunnel is formed by training the branches of two rows of trees to grow into each other to form an arched roof. Living pergolas and summerhouses can be formed by pleaching. After a few years, the supports are removed. Once established, clipping and pruning is generally required twice a year.

Plinth, Pedestal

A plinth is the base, usually made from a block of stone, that holds a statue, sculpture, urn, sundial, obelisk, column, or pedestal. A pedestal is set on the plinth and in turn, elevates a prized object. Often the words are used interchangeably, although technically, a pedestal goes on top of a plinth. They can be incorporated into a single piece.

Pedestals bring visibility and emphasis to the piece they display, an air of drama and importance. They can be quite majestic, with multiple levels, swags, inscriptions, and carvings, yet the best pedestals are foremost in service to the display of the piece being showcased. Pedestals must complement the piece, never overshadow it; they work especially well when designed together with the displayed work, as is often the case with sundials.

Even without a piece of art to show off, antique pedestals can be so beautiful in their own right that a gardener might want to install one as a work of art by itself, at least until the perfect work of art comes along. Dealers offer concrete and composite stone reproductions.

Installation can be a challenge, requiring below-grade footings and heavy equipment, but once established, a pedestal can remain in place for centuries.

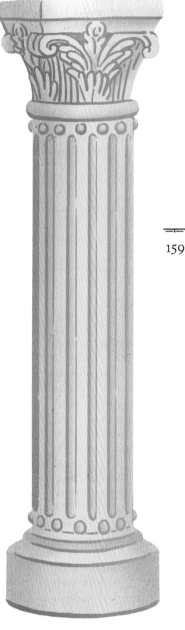

Potting Shed

A potting shed is a small outdoor structure built to hold tools, seeds, string, watering cans, stacks of flowerpots, wheelbarrows, and other necessities of the garden. It is outfitted with hooks, peg board, shelves, bins, and benches. There is space for planting seeds or potting up cuttings. Today's potting shed might also have a place to sit, with shelves for books. At least one window is traditional.

The potting sheds of the great walled kitchen gardens of nineteenth-century England were built close to the glasshouses of the garden so that gardeners could carry newly potted seeds and cuttings from one place to the other with little or no exposure to the weather. The main purpose of these sheds was as a place to work indoors, potting up plants, cleaning and sharpening tools, printing labels, readying plants for show, and making items such as nosegays. There was a stove or fireplace for heat. In those days, gardeners kept poisons (to kill everything from mice to aphids) locked in the office of the head gardener, or on a high shelf out of reach of young garden boys.

Potting sheds have become focal points in the garden, no longer relegated to the back corner.

Large kitchen gardens maintained separate tool sheds, but in smaller kitchen gardens, tools were stored in the potting shed. Orderliness was enforced, with each tool cleaned and returned to its assigned spot at the end of the work day. In 1894, Philadelphian Townsend Sharpless came up with the idea of drawing an outline of each tool on the wall where it was to hang. Many gardeners continue this practice today.

Later, in the twentieth century, smaller and simpler potting sheds used primarily as a place to store tools (including the now-ubiquitous lawn mower) were often hidden in the back corner of a property. Prefabricated sheds made of steel, wood, or vinyl came on the market.

Gardeners by nature have always cared about aesthetics and eschewed eyesores. They began rescuing sagging old outbuildings—such as sheep sheds, outhouses, and small garages—and, cleaning away cobwebs and debris, turned them into pretty potting sheds. They built new potting sheds with porches and stained-glass windows, creating personal spaces for gardening activities. Prefabricated garden sheds sported window boxes and cupolas.

Today, potting sheds have become focal points in the garden, no longer relegated to the back corner. They are approached via pretty, gently curved walks and surrounded by small gardens of their own. They are decorated with antiques or whimsical folk art. Herbs and flowers are hung to dry from the rafters. Tools are neatly arranged. Some are half-greenhouse, half-potting shed. Still, they are workhorses in the garden, providing crucial space for storage and key activities.

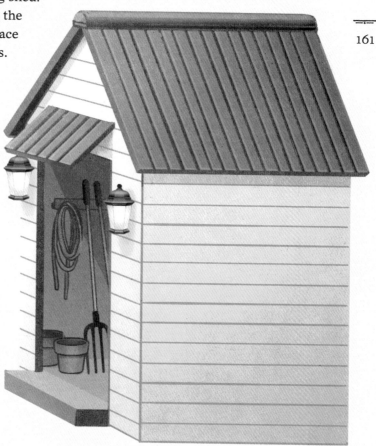

Railroad Garden

A railroad garden is an outdoor space that incorporates a model railroad scene into the landscaping. The scene usually includes tracks, buildings, bridges, tunnels, roads, and signs. In fact, experts advise that it is best to think of the railroad garden as a landscape. Suitable plants for such gardens include alpines, ground covers, succulents, heathers, and moss. Just as in a full-size garden, consideration is given to light and soil conditions. The land can be sculpted into hills and valleys with ponds.

The fascination with model trains appeared almost simultaneously with real trains. Originally made as promotional pieces for the railroads, they enchanted everyone who saw them. Too large to run indoors, and powered by steam, they were set up outdoors. Soon craftspeople were making models for themselves and for the estates of those who could afford them. They were particularly beloved in the UK and Germany.

In the twentieth century, the Lionel company, followed by American Flyer, popularized smaller model train sets for indoor use in the United States. In 1949, the Englishman R.E. Tustin published the manual *Garden Railways*, which explained the principles of outdoor gardening to scale for model railroads, but interest in the UK was declining and almost non-existent in America. Indoor trains were all the rage with young boys and girls. A fascination with outdoor garden railroads never completely disappeared, however. In 1969, a German toymaker introduced brightly colored plastic trains for the outdoors, reviving interest.

> **The fascination with model trains appeared almost simultaneously with real trains.**

Today, public railroad gardens can be found at numerous botanical gardens across America, including Longwood Gardens, the Chicago Botanic Garden, and the New Orleans Botanical Garden. They are also featured in numerous railroad museums and some zoos and private gardens which are open to the public. These include Castle Farms in Michigan and arboretums such as the Morris Arboretum at the University of Pennsylvania.

Home railroad gardeners point out that their gardens can be a shared activity for families whose interests may be far-ranging—from horticulture and miniature gardening to trains, model building, and history. Enthusiasts are served by numerous magazines, shows, and manufacturers. *Garden Railways* magazine has a horticultural editor on staff.

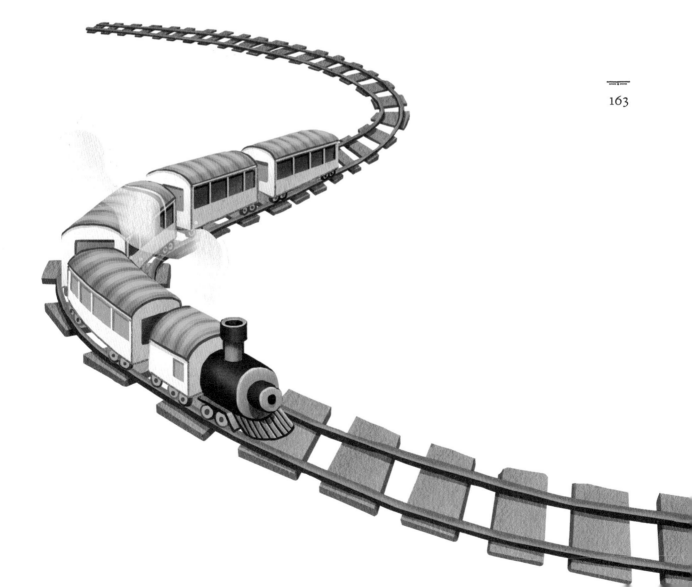

Rockery, Rock Garden

The origins of rock gardens go back in time to ancient China and Japan, but rather than focusing on plants, those gardens were truly gardens of rocks, with the attention on the rocks themselves and their symbolic representations of distant holy mountains. The rock garden movement that arose in the Victorian and Edwardian eras was more about plants, though the gardens themselves included arranged stones.

Beginning in the sixteenth century, tourists trekking above the tree line of the Alps during their summer holidays became enchanted with the views, the craggy rocks, the mountain peaks and most of all, the diminutive flowers and shrubs that flourished in the harsh conditions of such heights. The gardeners among them carried plants down from the peaks to grow at home, but met with little success. Though the trekkers stacked stones in their gardens to emulate the rocky highlands, the majority of transported plants shriveled and died.

The Austrian botanist Anton Kerner von Marilaun was one of the first to suggest that to successfully grow alpine plants, the gardener must replicate the plants' native environment. William Robinson made an excursion to the Alps in 1868 to observe plants in their natural habitat. By carefully "knocking and peeling" the roots bare, he saw, to his surprise, that many of the tiniest plants had extensive root systems, some as long as a yard, running beneath the rocks and scree. He concluded that most alpines, though appearing to grow on rocks, needed far more than a small pocket of soil in which to grow. Two years later, he published *Alpine Flowers for the English Garden*. Here, he disparaged the current rockeries and rock gardens, and gave his own best advice: the rock garden should be sited in open sun and be unseen from the formal parts of the garden; there should be no trees and no walks; rocks should be placed to look natural and to capture rain rather than let it cascade down; and the roots of the plants must be able to spread deep into the earth.

In 1919, Reginald Ferrier published *The English Rock Garden*, increasing the success of rock gardens, or rockeries as they were often called. Rock gardens were now very much in vogue on both sides of the Atlantic, with popularity at its highest in North America from the late nineteenth century to the first third of the twentieth century. The Pulham family, famous through several generations for the oversized rock gardens they engineered for their Victorian- and Edwardian-era clients, were acclaimed for the cliffs, waterfalls, and caves they built with enormous boulders of their own manufacture. Middle-class families made more modest rock gardens, sometimes a round affair in the middle of the front yard for all to see and admire. Beatrix Farrand designed a rock garden that stepped around the outside rim of the gardens at what is now Harkness Memorial State Park in Connecticut, with a winding path to scramble, a splashing pool, and spring bulbs.

The origins of rock gardens go back in time to ancient China and Japan . . . truly gardens of rocks.

The plant repertoire for rockeries expanded from alpines to include sedums, sempervivums, saxifrages, and small shrubs. Rock gardens planted solely with alpines were referred to as alpine gardens. Hillsides were covered with scree and planted. More writers argued and gave advice and opinions: rock gardens were low maintenance; rock gardens were high maintenance. Unsurprisingly, the style fell out of favor with designers. After a brief enthusiastic revival in the 1960s, they were again dismissed as gardening in bad taste.

Yet they continue to exert appeal. As in the past, rock gardens are a specialty garden within a larger garden. They have ardent devotees served by dedicated nurseries, suppliers, and organizations. There is a wealth of information available, ensuring, as much as any horticultural endeavor can ever be ensured, good results.

Roof Garden

In the areas of the world where snow does not fall and roofs are flat rather than pitched, people have used their rooftops as additional living space—including a space for plants—for thousands of years. In some ancient cultures, such as at Çatal Hüyük, in Turkey, the point of entry was the smoke outlet on the roof; there were no streets, alleys, or paths between houses, making the rooftops the outdoor connection between households. Ziggurats, massive Mesopotamian temples with stepped facades made of brick, were planted with trees and shrubs at each level, including the top. Ancient Greek and Roman women placed flowerpots on their rooftops every spring as part of the cult of Adonis. In Ming Dynasty China and later, a roof in Peking's famous Half-acre Garden served as a viewing terrace where guests enjoyed the moon at night and borrowed views of the White Dagoba on Kublai Khan's mound during the day.

Rooftop gardens were chic in New York City in the 1890s, as the price of land became prohibitive. At the turn of the century, the London department store Selfridges commissioned the creation of a roof garden on its flagship Oxford Street store, featuring a pergola, rock garden, pond, observation tower, and a putting green. Today, roof gardens grace hotels, office buildings, and high-rise residences in cities of even snowy temperate zones, adding value and status.

There are realities to roof gardens that can sometimes be daunting. Soil, raised beds, flowerpots, and plants themselves are heavy, especially after a rain or watering, making it is essential to first ascertain whether a roof is strong enough for the weight of a garden. An engineer and local authorities should be consulted. Roof gardens can also become very hot: the roof itself, nearby buildings, and the hard surfaces of the urban environment reflect heat. Unobstructed, they receive all-day sun and have little defense against wind. Additionally, planters should have drip trays or feet that raise them up, so that water does not damage the underlying surface.

Despite these challenges, a roof garden adds living space, improves air quality, and often increases the value of a property. A roof garden can be as simple as a tub of marigolds and tomatoes, or complex, with parterres, paths, arbors, raised beds, treillage, statuary, fountains, paths, a grill or firepit, and furniture. It can feature flowers, vegetables, or a combination of both.

Birds and butterflies will find their way to rooftops, and can be encouraged. Happily, marauding deer and rabbits cannot find their way to such heights. There have, however, been reports of squirrels and chipmunks poking azround in rooftop planters, upending bulbs, and causing havoc.

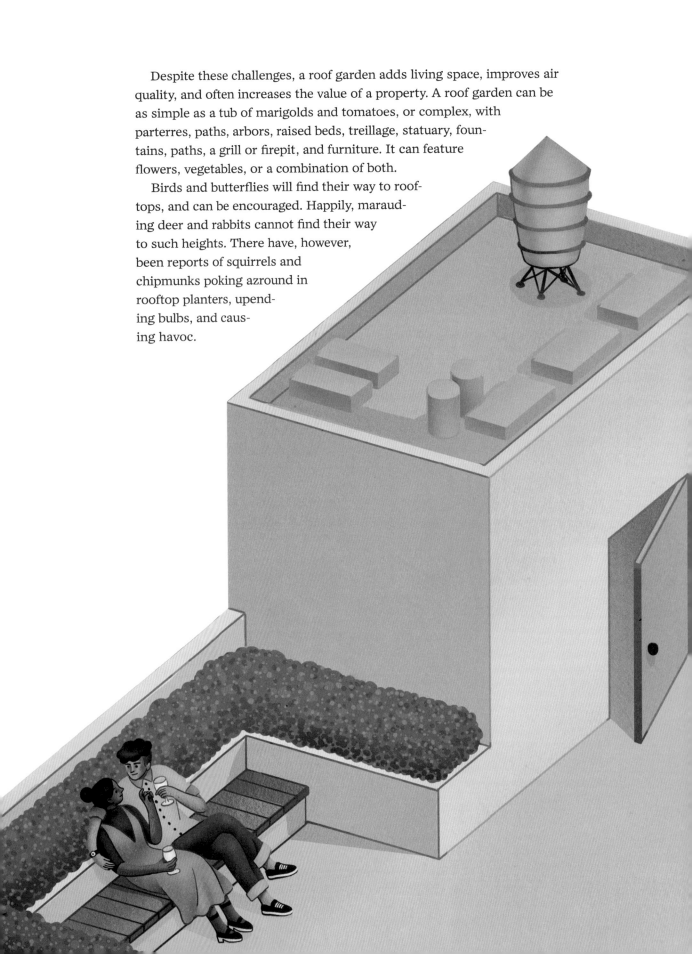

Living Roofs

All roof gardens are "green" and improve air quality. However, a green or living roof is more specifically a roof covered entirely with living plants such as grasses or sedum. In addition to improving air quality, this type of roof mitigates rainwater runoff and insulates the rooms below. Its main purpose is as a roof rather than a place for people.

Native Americans, and later, settlers from Europe, built sod houses with living grass roofs on the prairies of North America. The Vikings built turf houses in Iceland and Canada, where wood was scarce. The roofs were made of twigs covered with several layers of sod, topped with a layer of growing grass.

During the 1970s, amidst the back-to-the-land movement and widespread concerns about energy, interest in earth-sheltered housing surged, led by Cape Cod architect Malcolm Wells. These houses faced south for solar gain and, of course, had living, green roofs.

Novelist J.R.R. Tolkien's turf-covered hobbit houses were enchantingly interpreted for a movie set on a sheep and cattle farm in New Zealand. After being used for several movies, the set is now a heavily visited tourist attraction. The little hobbit houses with living grass roofs are the main draw, and similar turf-roofed houses grace gardens throughout the world.

New technology has made green roofs planted with grasses, succulents, sedums, herbs, and wildflowers not quite mainstream, perhaps, but certainly beautiful and practical. They are no longer considered alternative, nor are they exclusive to houses whose walls are also turf. Rooftop meadows are appearing in cities, on college campuses, and in industrial parks. Reliable waterproof membranes, lightweight growing materials, sensitive designs, buildings with load-bearing capabilities, plus the recognition of the environmental benefits have made this ancient concept a tool for helping to ameliorate climate change.

Room

By separating a garden into distinct areas, or outdoor rooms, it is possible to combine different styles that would not otherwise work together, as one cannot be seen from the other. Rooms make a garden look and feel larger than it is. Because visitors cannot see everything with one sweeping glance, they are drawn to wander and explore, thus spending more time in the garden.

With rooms, you can plant for different peak periods. Gertrude Jekyll planted parts of her own garden at Munstead Wood this way. Her autumn garden overflowed with michaelmas daisies (asters)—stunning in season and the subject of one of Margery Allingham's paintings, but not so exciting the rest of the year. She could have spread them around, planting each border for the modern notion of four-season interest, but she would have sacrificed the spectacular punch of hundreds of michaelmas daisies burst into bloom all at once.

Like the rooms of a house, the rooms of a garden must work together.

Vita Sackville-West divided her beloved garden at Sissinghurst into ten rooms. She used what she called "inherited walls," the old brick remains of the castle she and Harold Nicolson purchased, combined with yew hedges that they planted, to create her rooms. Masterful gardener that she was, she designed the layout so that a glimpse from one room into the next framed an enticing vignette, luring visitors for a closer look. Because she wrote extensively about her gardens in her books and her weekly column for the *Observer*, and many people visited and continue to visit Sissinghurst, her rooms have influenced generations of gardeners.

Rooms are delineated with hedges, walls, fences, the sides of buildings, or trellises. The law of significant enclosure (designers do call it a law), tells us that a three-to-one ratio of distance to height is ideal. This means that the height of the hedge or wall should be one third the distance across the space, in order to create a comfortable sense of enclosure.

Rooms as an organizing principle are employed in both formal and informal gardens, lending order and intrigue to the landscape. Paths and openings connect one room to another. Though the rooms may be very different, there needs to be some continuity or narrative to pull everything together. Like the rooms of a house, the rooms of a garden must work together. This can be accomplished in a number of ways, such as repeating a few plant types in each room, maintaining a similar color palate, and using similar paths or hedging material throughout.

Scarecrow

The first scarecrows were people. Being a scarecrow was even a job during the early Middle Ages. Usually boys, but also men, or old men who could no longer do heavy work like plowing, would spend all day watching for crows and shout and shoo them away from the field crops and fruit trees. As late as the twentieth century, human scarecrows performed this duty in rural and ecologically sensitive regions of England.

But it is the straw-and-old-clothes scarecrow we speak of here, made of ragged coveralls or jeans and a flannel shirt, or an old dress and apron, stuffed with straw, a head made of a pillow case or piece of sheet and also stuffed with straw; all topped with a straw hat and held upright on a stake or set to relax on an old chair. The construction of a scarecrow invites innovation and resourcefulness, and, often, humor, satire, or political comment.

A scarecrow might be outfitted with shiny tin pie pans that move in the wind, a scary mask for a face, empty cans strung together so they rattle and clank, or even a hidden radio. The entire scarecrow might be affixed to his stake so that he or she sways slightly from side to side. The idea is to give the scarecrow enough animation to surprise hungry avian thieves.

Traditional scarecrows in India are made by setting a broken or discarded pot upside down on a post. A face is then painted on the pot.

Culturally, scarecrows or straw men serve as metaphors for something purposely fake that can be knocked down. They appear in literature and film: in Shakespeare's plays, in Edmund Spencer's *The Faerie Queene*, and in *The Wizard of Oz* books and movies. Their usefulness in the garden and field as a deterrent to birds has been debated for centuries. Nevertheless, they remain an important expression in the garden, especially the vegetable garden, an irresistible piece of horticultural folk art. Towns host scarecrow festivals, inviting visitors to go from garden to garden to see the year's straw creations.

Shrubbery

A shrubbery is an area of the garden that is densely planted with hardy shrubs. It can be a wide and thick border, a broad hedge, a large island, or a plot of shrubs laced with paths.

A glade might be enclosed by a thick shrubbery, lending a sense of secrecy and sanctuary. Most often the shrubs include a mix of flowering and evergreen specimens, but a single species can be used. A well-planned shrubbery offers four seasons of interest. It is easier to care for than mixed or perennial borders, requiring only occasional pruning.

A rhododendron shrubbery might cover a hillside, the understory of a forest, or an old field. Typically, paths would meander through the collection, engaging visitors. At Bowood House and Gardens in the UK, over thirty acres are devoted to rhododendrons mixed with azaleas and magnolias, underplanted with bluebells and accessed by a series of walks.

In the nineteenth century, English landscape gardeners favored picturesque shrubberies with winding gravel paths that led visitors away from the house. Here, unseen and unheard by others, wandering guests could speak privately while enjoying the beauty of the shrubs.

Gertrude Jekyll used shrubberies as a transition between the rest of the garden and the woods. This is still an effective scheme, with the added benefit of attracting wildlife such as songbirds.

For the aging gardener no longer able to spend long hours on his or her knees weeding or with back bent deadheading perennials, converting borders to shrubberies offers the opportunity to continue gardening. Shrubberies also appeal to time-pressed young families managing busy careers and raising young children. But even gardeners without physical or time constraints find a shrubbery a valuable enhancement to the garden.

Stairs

Almost as long as gardeners have been dealing with sloped ground, they have included stairs in their gardens. Ancient cultures associated heights with gods, heaven, and spiritual enlightenment. The Chinese have revered Mount Tai (or Taishan) for more than 2000 years. Nearly 7000 stone steps, with temples and statuary along the way, ascend this holy mountain that Confucius himself climbed. Mesopotamians built ziggurats, great stepped pyramids, from 2200 to 500 BCE. Strabo tells us that the pinnacle of the Hanging Gardens of Babylon was reached by a steep staircase.

Romans, who gardened on sloping terrain but preferred flat ground, made cut stone stairs to connect their many terraces. Later, the gardeners of the Italian Renaissance raised grand garden staircases to an art form, influencing the gardens of France and England.

Gertrude Jekyll believed that shallow stone steps in a garden, two feet wide with five-inch risers, conveyed a sense of welcome. She specified plants, seats, landings, and basins of water, ensuring leisurely pleasure. Never, however, were plants to "invade the middle space." Steps were an important design feature of her signature sunken gardens. Her design partner Edwin Lutyens was famous for his half-moon stone steps, such as those he created at Great Dixter.

Formal or rustic, stairs add drama and energy to the garden.

Stairs continue to play an important role in gardens in the twenty-first century, connecting decks and porches to gardens, tying levels and terraces together, and accessing hills and slopes. For safety, they are subject to local building codes specifying railings, number of landings, riser heights and stair widths, tread depths, surface treatments, and in cold areas, footings. The most important safety consideration is that steps be consistent. Risers of varying heights cause stumbles and falls. Stairs should be wobble free and also drain well.

Stairs are made of cut stone, field stones, bricks, pressure-treated wood, logs, turf, or combinations of materials. Risers can be faced with tiles. Gravel can be used on the treads. Formal or rustic, stairs add drama and energy to the garden. They create a sense of movement, pulling the visitor onward. If they are broad enough, they provide an extra place to sit or display pots. Curved stairs descending into a sunken terrace can double as amphitheater seats for poetry readings and musical performances.

Stake, Cage, Teepee

As the domestication of plants advanced, gardeners and farmers realized that many grew better when held off the ground. We know from ancient Egyptian tomb art that grapes were grown up stakes, with the vine itself forming a bower from one stake to another. Later, the Egyptians made aerial supports between the stakes, creating grape arbors.

Ancient Roman and Chinese gardeners grew fruit and vines against walls. The Chinese also grew some plants between fences for support. Garden historian Anthony Huxley writes that the first evidence of supports used for herbaceous plants and shrubs appears in the literature and art of the Middle Ages. He also tells us that during the first visit of Christopher Columbus to the West Indies, Columbus observed supports made of three or more sticks lashed to form a sort of wigwam for pumpkins and squash, a support which was soon widely used in Europe. Today, teepees are used for vines such as pole beans, morning glories, sweet peas, and clematis. They can be found in informal flower gardens and cottage gardens as well as the vegetable garden.

Pea sticks (stakes named for their original use: supporting peas) were made from coppiced trees, and from branches of hazel, beech, willow, and hawthorn trees that gardeners gathered from nearby woods and hedgerows and cut into sticks. They were also woven into round and square cages.

In the seventeenth century, with the arrival of tulips in Europe, growers made special stakes of wire with a loop to hold the stem upright. Utilitarian, they were meant to show off the flower head and were soon used for other florists' flowers.

It was the Victorians, with their love of ornamentation and curlicues, who made fancy stakes, often meant to be as visible as the plants they held. These had umbrella-shaped "trainer" stakes for standard roses, iron stakes with finials on top, and peony rings. By the mid-nineteenth century, John Claudius Loudon was expounding in books and magazines on iron stakes of various lengths, the proper way to stake trees, and the benefits of stakes made of beech, hazel, and willow. He berated sloppy staking.

Stakes are meant to be unseen in the flower border, an important but invisible garden element. They are the hidden scaffolding that keeps floppy plants from flopping. Some gardeners weave their pea sticks into basket-like supports, making an art of it. Others stick with straight stakes. There are a variety of metal stakes, ring supports, and cages powder-coated green for invisibility. The writer and designer Margery Fish called a garden where staking was neglected "a depressing sight."

There is no need or benefit to hiding stakes in the food garden, where the practice of supporting plants began so many millennia ago. Here, stakes have a job to do. Tomatoes benefit from being staked with at least one tall and sturdy wood or bamboo pole, often two or more. Round, galvanized metal tomato cages are offered for sale in nearly every garden center and hardware store. These range from thirty to over fifty inches tall and have three supporting rings plus a ring on top. They are useful for tomatoes, cucumbers, and other vining plants. A host of other cages and tomato supports are also available, with new improvements arriving annually. There are galvanized metal cages which are square, and tomato towers and ladders made of powder-coated steel. Green steel blends in with leaves and highly visible red steel is reputed to enhance the production of tomatoes.

Statue, Sculpture

A statue is a realistic three-dimensional representation of a human or animal—including gods, mythological figures, and monsters—usually large and made of metal or stone. Statues punctuate and decorate a garden, offer associations with history and mythology, and add a layer of complexity to the landscape. They are often modeled and cast, so can be reproduced. Smaller versions are known as figurines or statuettes.

A sculpture can be either abstract or representational of any subject and made of various materials. It is an original work of art and can be stationary or kinetic. A statue is a sculpture, but not all sculptures are statues.

Both have a long association with gardens. Garden statuary began with terra-cotta and stone gods in ancient temple gardens in the Fertile Crescent, in ancient Egypt, and in China and India. Finely crafted marble statues of gods and emperors adorned ancient Roman gardens, courtyards, and public spaces. Later, statues of Diana, Venus, Hercules, Neptune, Apollo, and the many Caesars graced Italian Renaissance gardens. Here they were admired, copied, and sometimes even stolen by other European gardeners, especially the English.

The work needs to be large enough to make an impression in the landscape.

The English climate was less suited to stone than Italy, as lichen and moss could obscure details and the freeze-thaw cycles of winter could cause damage, but gardeners discovered that lead held up to the cold and damp very well. Shepherds, shepherdesses, putti, cherubs, children, lions, horses, and herons as well as the gods and goddesses of Roman mythology were placed at the ends of axes, in niches in hedges, in pools of water, at the edges of lawns—wherever they could draw the eye and be enjoyed. Busts also appeared.

Victorians reproduced many classic statues. Identical Pans and putti and cherubs decorated their gardens.

Sculpture gardens are conceived as outdoor galleries: settings for multiple pieces of art. In the sixteenth century, Pier Francesco Orsini created his magnificent and highly unusual sculpture garden in Bomarzo, Italy, filling it with gargantuan monsters, demons, and ghoulish creatures carved in situ from local soft stone. Here were snarling winged dragons, an ogre with a gaping mouth large enough for a person to enter, a tilted house, a giant tearing another apart and other fascinating and darkly beautiful horrors sculpted of stone. After Orsini's death, his surrealistic garden was neglected and swallowed by the forest, where it lay hidden beneath moss and tangled growth for centuries until Salvador Dali discovered and filmed it. Today, visitors come to the garden from all over the world.

Sculpture gardens today are made to show a collection of sculpted works, to present a changing exhibit of sculpture, or a combination of the two. Outstanding public sculpture gardens include the Hirshhorn Museum and Sculpture Garden at the Smithsonian, in Washington, DC, and the Fran and Ray Stark Sculpture Garden at the Getty Center in Los Angeles.

Whether statuary or sculpture is being chosen for a garden, the work needs to be large enough to make an impression in the landscape. A gardener needs to consider what sort of base or foundation is required, how the elements will interact with the material, how light falls on the piece at different times of day, and how the piece will be approached and viewed. Sadly, in some locations, the potential for theft needs to be considered. However, being able to add a piece of favorite art to the garden, and siting it where both the garden and the artwork are enhanced, is worth the effort.

Stumpery

A stumpery is a collection of tree stumps that have been gathered, set in proximity to each other, and arranged so that the roots are exhibited in the air. Compost or soil is placed in pockets and around the stumps and planted with shade lovers such as ferns. Lichens and moss are encouraged. Logs and driftwood might be added for interest. Stumperies are usually tucked into a cleared corner of a woodland garden and offer a visual and sensual surprise to the visitor. They have an ethereal, preternatural feel about them. They attract wildlife such as toads, frogs, newts, insects, and small mammals, but you almost expect to see a circle of fairies appear beneath the twists and folds of the roots.

The largest stumpery open to the public is the half-acre stumpery at the twenty-two-acre Rhododendron Species Botanical Garden in Tacoma, Washington. It boasts 140 Douglas fir stumps and logs thoughtfully planted with ferns and other plants collected from around the world.

Edward William Cooke, a landscape and marine painter and gardener, created the first known stumpery in 1856 at Biddulph Grange, in Staffordshire, UK, with his friend and fellow gardener James Bateman, who owned the estate. Made of enormous, ancient oak stumps placed close together, the roots entangled and piled as high as ten feet, the collection was planted with ferns, vines, and sprawlers. A sunken

Stumperies are usually tucked into a cleared corner of a woodland garden and offer a visual and sensory surprise.

The
Royal Stumpery

One of the most well-known private stumperies is at Highgrove Royal Gardens in the UK, made by Prince Charles and inspired by the stumperies of the Victorian era. A well-known thatched tree house called Hollyrood House can be found there, as well as artfully placed, upturned sweet chestnut stumps, ferns, and a prized Natural Collection of broad-leaved and large hostas. The Stumpery also features the Wall of Gifts, which showcases a display of architectural stone collected by the Prince.

Natural structures include two classical temples that are made of green oak but are sculpted to look like stone. The sculpture Goddess of the Wood sits at their base.

path traversed the stumpery. It inspired the construction of stumperies throughout the second half of the nineteenth century and attracts many visitors today.

Gardeners can often obtain stumps from local arborists who would otherwise dispose of them as waste. Three stumps are enough for a small stumpery. Over the years, the stumps will decay, changing in appearance and adding to the romance. Ultimately, they will become part of the garden floor, making room for more stumps. Once considered an oddity or topic of conversation, stumperies are gaining favor again as gardeners embrace their unconventional beauty and environmental benefits, such as shelter for small wildlife.

Sundial

The first timekeeping devices were sundials. Because they must be placed out in the open in a sunny spot to work, they have a long association with gardens. At least as early as 3500 BCE, people made sundials by thrusting a stick into the ground—a gnomon—and noting the length of the shadow. Babylonians, Egyptians, Greeks, Romans, and Chinese relied on, and in some cases improved upon, the sundial. For centuries after the invention of mechanical clocks in the fourteenth century, sundials were used to check for accuracy. Ancient Greeks and Chinese developed the armillary sphere sundial.

Sundials were prevalent in the gardens of Tudor England, in early American gardens, and in Colonial Revival gardens. They were also popular during the Arts and Crafts Movement. The sundial itself, consisting of the dial and gnomon, was made of a metal such as lead, brass, copper, bronze, or cast iron. It was elevated on a baluster or pedestal of stone. Gertrude Jekyll recommended that the pedestal should itself be elevated on a step or platform. Armillary sphere sundials were favored by the upper gentry.

The Tudors, whose geometric gardens included raised beds, paths, and an enclosing wall, liked to place a sundial in the middle of a knot garden, as a focal point. Nineteenth-century American merchants and gentlemen farmers often placed a sundial in the center of the main axis of their gardens. Writer and landscape designer Andrew Jackson Downing recommended putting a sundial in the middle of a flower parterre or along a walkway. In the garden-making years at the end of the nineteenth century and beginning of the twentieth, when "old-fashioned" gardens were at their height, a sundial was almost a requirement.

Particularly charming were the poetic mottoes related to the passing of time that were inscribed on the pedestal, the dial itself, or both. These were often taken from classical literature, written by the owner, or copied from a book of appropriate mottoes and rhymes. Many were melancholic reflections on mortality or wistful observations on life such as the following.

Hours fly,
Flowers die,
New days,
New ways,
Pass by;
Love stays.

—*from a sundial in Saratoga, New York*

Today, we most often find sundials on the grounds of historic houses and in herb gardens and public gardens. They should be placed in a sunny, level spot of the garden that makes design sense, such as where paths cross, or in the center, with the gnomon facing celestial north. You can achieve reasonable accuracy by setting a sundial out at noon so that the arm casts its shadow on the twelve. The best days to do this are April 15, June 15, September 1, or December 24, when sundial time and clock time agree, but you can do it any day of the year and then make any needed correction on one of these days.

Sundials convey the essence of time passing as the shadow moves across the dial. Gardens are made of the passage of time. Gardens and sundials tell the same story—which may be why sundials continue to exert strong appeal as a garden element.

Sunken Garden

A sunken (or sunk as they were also called) garden lies below ground level on at least two sides, and more often on all four. It can be deep or shallow. A sunken garden has walls made of earth or masonry, such as stone or brick. It might have required heavy equipment and much earth moving to create, or only a hand shovel. It might be sited in a natural depression within an old foundation. It can be attached to a house, or set out in the landscape.

Ancient Egyptians and Romans enjoyed the pretty and convenient shelter from the heat of the Mediterranean summer sun that these spaces provided. Herod made a sunken garden in the southern wing of his winter palace in Jericho and filled it with potted plants. The Zunis made sunken gardens, square depressions with clay or adobe walls, that helped conserve water in their arid farmland. The Inca made mountaintop sunken gardens. Italian sunken gardens, such as the garden of Flora to the east of the sixteenth-century Villa Torrigiani, influenced garden making throughout England and the United States.

Sunken gardens have graced the pleasure grounds of kings and queens. Wealthy landowners added them to their estates and invited guests to admire them. They were incorporated in public parks on both sides of the Atlantic. They appeared in botanical gardens as diverse as the Durban Botanic Gardens in South Africa, where the sunken garden is planted with annuals, and the Desert Botanical Garden in Phoenix, Arizona, where the sunken garden seems to spiral downward.

The Zunis made . . . square depressions with clay or adobe walls that helped conserve water in their arid farmland.

Sunken gardens were a widespread feature of Arts and Crafts gardens, favored especially by Gertrude Jekyll and her followers. They were de rigueur in turn-of-the-century American gardens of even moderate size. They usually featured a small pool or fountain in the center, and a sundial at one end.

Public gardens which include sunken gardens invariably list them as an important and unique feature. Noted designers working today, such as interior designer and author Bunny Williams, who created a much-photographed sunken garden for her home in the northwestern hills of Connecticut, have also embraced

the form. Nevertheless, sunken gardens are far less prevalent in the twenty-first century than they were a hundred or so years ago. This is beginning to change, though. Like Edna St. Vincent Millay did at her home, Steepletop, gardeners are converting the stone foundations of old barns into sunken gardens. Though it is unfortunate that so many barns are falling into disuse and decay, when lost, their foundations provide the creative gardener with an opportunity to add an exciting dimension to the garden.

Barring the availability of an old stone foundation, it is still possible to add a sunken garden with a bit of excavation. The garden needn't be more than a few feet deep, especially if the upper perimeter is planted with shrubs. Alice Morse Earle, writing in her best-selling book *Old Time Gardens*, published in 1901, recommended excavating two or three feet and adding a two-foot brick wall above, giving a feel of enclosure when inside. She wanted stone steps leading down to the garden, interior flower borders and a pane of grass in the center. Her advice is still worthy.

Swing, Hammock

Swings made of a board suspended from an overhead tree branch by two ropes have appeared in art and gardens for thousands of years. Swings are shown in Middle Eastern art as early as 1450 BCE. Classic red and black vases from ancient Greece feature women and children on swings. A charming terra-cotta sculpture made in Mexico circa 300–900 CE portrays two figures side by side on a swing. Late eighteenth-century and early nineteenth-century paintings, most famously *The Swing*, painted around 1767 by Jean Honoré Fragonard, show women on swings surrounded by lush greenery, garden statues, and flowers.

Identical swings hang in gardens today. But we also have lawn swings, tandem swings, strombrellas, and gliders. The American front porch, which came into prominence in the mid-nineteenth century, was often furnished with a bench-like swing with a back. Cushions and pillows added to the comfort. Wooden four-passenger tandem swings, with two seats facing each other, were offered with the option of sun shade or awning in the first years of the twentieth century. These were placed on the lawn. There were also side-by-side, two-person tandem swings for the lawn.

In the 1930s, several patents were issued for a glider mechanism which led to the glider swing. A glider moved gently back and forth, more restful than a swing or rocker. After World War II, Ed Warmack, an Arkansas manufacturer, began making brightly colored, stamped-steel chairs and gliders. He produced cantilevered gliders (that looked like two of his clamshell chairs side by side) as well as a more substantial stamped-steel glider that looked more like a metal couch.

The strombrella is a one- or two-person swing with a roof, rather like a self-contained gazebo-swing all in one. It does not take up much space in the garden and can be quite charming.

Hammocks come to us from Central America, where they were made of bark or fiber and used for sleeping more than a thousand years ago. It is believed that Columbus is the first European to see a hammock, which he encountered in the Bahamas and brought back to Spain. They were quickly adopted by sailors who made them of canvas rather than fiber. Navies worldwide used hammocks right up through World War II.

Nineteenth-century artists Gustave Courbet, Theodore Robinson, Winslow Homer, and many others, followed by twentieth-century artists such as Jessie Wilcox Smith and Diego Rivera produced paintings depicting women in hammocks, alone or together, often reading. Also portrayed were children, or women and children together, in hammocks. Suspended from trees in idealized forest and garden settings, the spacious hammocks and their inhabitants convey a sense of joy. The abundance of such paintings gives us an idea of how deeply the hammock had entered the psyche of Americans and Europeans, and its importance in gardens.

Classic red and black vases from ancient Greece feature women and children on swings.

Though fundamentally unchanged for thousands of years, swings and hammocks are now available in a variety of styles and materials. They are used to best advantage when tucked into a quiet, secluded area of the garden where they can be enjoyed peacefully.

Topiary, Standard

A topiary is a tree or shrub that has been clipped, pruned, and trained into an artificial and decorative shape such as a globe, cube, obelisk, lollipop, spiral, animal, or person. Box and yew are the most common plants used, but rosemary, myrtle, and other small-leaved evergreens also work. Movable topiaries are grown in clay pots. Larger topiaries are grown as formal accents or as the whimsical raison d'être of an entire space.

Known widely as the oldest and most extensive topiary gardens, Levens Hall in the Lake District of England has over 100 topiaries, some 300 years old, including topiary chess pieces, peacocks, umbrellas, abstract forms, and even a topiary jug of Morocco ale. It is a veritable living-sculpture garden. The gardens were begun in the late seventeenth century and have survived the ravages of changing fashions in the garden world.

> Box and yew are the most common plants used, but rosemary, myrtle, and other small-leaved evergreens also work.

Indeed, topiary has gone in and out of fashion since the Ancient Egyptians first clipped shrubs for their gardens. After being introduced to topiary by his good friend Cneus (also spelled Gnaius or Caius) Matius, the Emperor Augustus became so enchanted with the art form that he set off a fad among Romans who sculpted ships and hunting scenes from yew. Even Pliny the Elder employed topiary on his Tuscan estate. Except in monasteries, where topiary continued to be grown, interest waned after the collapse of the empire. It was renewed in Italy during the Renaissance, becoming synonymous with the Italian garden style. During the seventeenth century, known as the golden age of topiary, the clipped plants decorated gardens throughout Europe, especially in England, France, Holland, Denmark, Germany, and of course, Italy. In France, led by André Le Nôtre, topiary was geometric. The Dutch, followed by the English, embraced figurative topiary. Then, with the rise of the landscape movement, topiary again fell out of fashion, much of it allowed to grow out or ruthlessly removed. Rural cottage gardeners, however, oblivious of the latest fashion, never put their clippers away. The nineteenth century saw a revival, particularly during the years of the Victorians. Topiary enjoyed another revival in the twentieth century under the aegis of such gardeners as Vita Sackville-West and Lawrence Johnston. Even Walt Disney's theme parks instituted topiary figures.

During the 1980s in South Carolina, Pearl Fryar took a three-minute lesson in topiary at a local nursery, and with a step ladder and a hedge trimmer, began creating his own topiaries. At first, he just wanted to beautify his home, but soon he wanted to show that an African American could win the Yard-of-the-Month Award from the garden club. Often working with sickly plants that the nursery discarded, he created a wonderland of topiary on his three acres, eventually planting and sculpting 500 trees and shrubs. Not only did he win, but today, the Pearl Fryar Topiary Garden is under the protection of the Garden Conservancy and sees more than 5000 visitors a year.

Creating a topiary takes time and patience. Plants must be grown to maturity and clipped with regularity. For elaborate shapes, branches must be trained with wires. Large, mature topiaries send gardeners up ladders. Yet, the art has become easier. Topiary forms are available for training plants. Even ivies are trained into shapes. Potted, ready-trained topiaries are offered by nurseries and garden centers. Home owners can now easily flank their front doors or patio steps with topiaries that, already having achieved the desired shape, require only an annual or twice-yearly trim. Topiaries will go in and out of fashion, but as history shows, they will never disappear.

A standard is a tree or herbaceous perennial such as a rose or geranium that has been trained to have a single stem. Beatrix Farrand was fond of heliotrope standards, with their fragrant heads of purple flowers. She liked to use them as accents. Standard, or tree, roses were developed in Germany in the late eighteenth century. They were made by grafting a rose bush onto the roots and stem of a hardy rootstock and, like today, grown in pots or planted directly in the garden.

Topography

The earth is not flat. Neither are most garden properties. Beginning a garden, one is faced with surface irregularities. The slopes, hillocks, streambeds, and hollows must all be taken into account. These terrain features can be incorporated into designs, or, with shovels or earth-moving equipment, they can be changed into preferred surface elements. One can terrace a hillside, flatten a hummock, scoop out earth to make a pond, drain a swamp, or change the course of a stream.

The human urge to change the earth's topography dates back to prehistory and continues to the present. At the beginning of the current era, the Nazca people created mysterious geoglyphs of hummingbirds, lizards, trapezoids, spiders, and swirls across Peru by excavating lines as many as thirty miles long. Prior to that, perhaps as many as 4000 years ago, an unknown people created huge earthen mounds shaped like whales, pumas, birds, and ducks in the same area.

The terraced rice paddies of the Philippines, China, and other Asian countries date back 2000 years. They are a complex system of terraces and water channels that work together to make up an integrated system of agriculture. The topography has been altered by building retaining walls, then infilling with gravel to create a flat terrace which is flooded. These terraces require constant maintenance.

The Chinese liked to create mounds, or false mountains in their gardens, which Marco Polo admired when he visited. He estimated that the artificial mound in the summer palace garden of Kublai Khan at Xanadu was a mile high. It was made from earth that was dug to make a garden lake. Modern experts estimate it was a thousand feet.

> Beginning a garden . . . the slopes, hillocks, streambeds, and hollows must all be taken into account.

The eighteenth-century landscape architect Capability Brown sculpted serpentine lakes and undulating hills, moved mature trees, planted forests, dug ha-has, and transformed the landscapes of his clients. The construction of Central Park in New York, designed by Frederick Law Olmstead and Calvert Vaux, entailed draining swamps, dynamiting granite, digging tunnels, bringing in 18,500 cubic yards of soil from great distances, not to mention removing the people who lived on the site, including Irish farmers and the free African American residents of the village of Seneca. By the time of the Country House era that swept the UK and United States at the end of the nineteenth and beginning of the twentieth centuries, wealthy landowners were merrily terracing their estates and otherwise rearranging their topographies.

Today, we are more aware of and sensitive to the environmental impact of altering topography. We value wetlands. We are aware that if we change the course of a river, we are not just changing the topography of our gardens, but of everyone whose property lies downriver. Building hills and leveling hills changes the drainage patterns of a property. Before beginning such projects, we must get permits from the government, perhaps pay for engineering studies, and consult with our neighbors.

Many gardeners have chosen instead to embrace what nature offers and work with it, or as the eighteenth-century poet Alexander Pope admonished, "Consult the genius of the land." They seek to incorporate the topography, the *genius loci*, into their design, and even let it dictate the plan.

Joe Eck and the late Wayne Winterrowd purchased the land where they made their much-visited garden, North Hill, because it sloped and had a seasonal stream. "These essential variables of hill, wood, and stream have controlled the character of the garden from the beginnings . . . The land imposed its will, and in only a few cases have we thought it wise to alter what it offered us," they write in *A Year at North Hill: Four Seasons in a Vermont Garden*.

Theodate Pope Riddle, faced with the challenge of a large natural depression in the hilltop land where she had designed Hill-Stead, a spacious colonial revival home and working farm in Farmington, Connecticut, used the depression to make a sunken garden for her mother. Surrounded by stone walls with an oblong summer house and sundial in the center, the garden was a favorite spot for entertaining. Today it is the setting for summer poetry readings.

Gordon Hayward, garden designer and author, writing about sites with outcrops of bedrock, advocates working with what you have, to "see the fundamental, elemental beauty." He has designed gardens with bedrock and boulders in a number of creative ways, leaving the lichen-covered rocks to speak for themselves, using native plants, and tying an outcrop of bedrock to the rest of the landscape with boulders.

Whether we are changing the topography in our garden, keeping it as-is, or making modest changes while leaving much as we find it—terracing a hill perhaps, or creating a pond in a boggy area—topography is an underlying element of all gardens, influencing the success of the plants and the architecture.

Trellis, Treillage, Lattice Work

Lattice work, slats of wood or metal that have been interwoven to form regular, usually diamond or square, openings, has long been a part of gardening. A trellis is lattice work in a frame. Treillage is the overall term.

At its most basic and simplest, a trellis is for supporting plants. A trellis can be placed in a border and entwined with roses, set in a raised bed in the vegetable garden for the cucumbers, or doubled and erected as a pair on each side of a front door, draped with trumpet vine or Dutchman's pipe. Such trellises are commercially available in metal, wood, and vinyl. Or, if you possess basic carpentry skills, you can purchase a bit of lattice and build a trellis yourself.

Treillage is depicted in first-century Roman frescoes and Medieval tapestries. Sixteenth-century German lawyer Paul Hentzner exclaimed over "delicious gardens" with "groves ornamented with trellis work," when describing what he saw in England during the reign of Queen Elizabeth I. When Pierre le Nôtre—grandfather of André le Nôtre, who designed the gardens of Versailles—applied for the job of master gardener in the Paris Guild, he submitted his designs for treillage to show his qualifications. He got the job. His grandson used treillage in bold and fanciful ways, influencing gardeners for generations. Treillage was a key component of grand French gardens during the eighteenth and nineteenth centuries.

A trellis is lattice work in a frame. Treillage is the overall term.

Elsie de Wolfe, the glamorous interior decorator best known for covering the walls of her clients' homes with masses of treillage, thus giving their living and dining rooms a suggestion of the outdoors, filled her personal garden in Versailles with treillage. She used it as her "high garden fence," for growing vines, and at the entrance to her garden.

Perhaps the most romantic use of a trellis is against a house or outbuilding wall. Grace Tabor, a prolific garden writer and landscape architect of the early twentieth century, advocated placing trellises horizontally above the first-floor windows of a house, with one or two vertical trellises joining them to the ground so that a profusion of vines could embrace the house.

Trellis work is remarkably versatile. It can be used to enclose or form lavish curved garden alcoves or the sides of long pergolas, creating what Gertrude Jekyll called somewhat disparagingly, "elaborate pavilions and arcades of complicated treillage." She went on to bemoan the fact that these "edifices" had been often left unplanted, so that they might not be marred, and rejoiced that "saner" use of treillage was being practiced. By saner, she meant planted with vines or espaliered trees. Included in her book on garden ornaments are photos of an oak trellis for fruit trees placed at the back of a garden, and a charming little building with latticed sides ready for planting.

A row of trellises, attached or set a few feet apart, planted with vines, is a wonderful way to divide a garden into separate rooms. It gives an immediate effect, as opposed to the years a hedge takes to reach maturity. This works well in a small urban garden where one wants to create the illusion of more space, and also in rambling country gardens where some intimacy is desired. A valuable trait of treillage is that it can visually expand or contract the sense of a garden, depending upon how it is used.

Skipping Tabor's horizontal trellises, and simply placing one or two vertically

against a wall is also charming, if more common. Planted with vines, it clothes the house in summer and adds winter interest when the leaves have fallen. Some adventurous gardeners even rest a trellis upon their roof to extend the reach and cover of their plants.

Care must be taken to not damage house exteriors. It is best to leave a couple of inches of air space and, if at all possible, make it easy to detach the trellis by the top, so you can lay it down without disturbing the vines when it is time to paint the house.

Treillage fits formal and informal, urban and country, large and small gardens. It has many applications, from the skin of an elaborate pavilion to a support for the season's pole beans. It offers enclosure yet does not restrict the view. Treillage is solid enough to serve as a wall or fence, but it is airy.

Trough Garden

For centuries, English farmers used hand-carved stone troughs made of local granite, limestone, or sandstone to water and feed their livestock. They were often long, narrow, and rectangular, but square, round, and oval troughs were also made, each carved from a single block of stone. Set near a barn or along the edge of a field, in a stone wall between fields so that animals on both sides could have access, they were sturdy and functional. Large troughs were for horses and cattle, small for sheep or goats. Around the middle of the nineteenth century, iron troughs became prevalent, and many old stone troughs were abandoned.

Twentieth-century gardeners were enchanted with the rustic beauty of ancient stone troughs, often encrusted with lichen, and adopted them for alpine and succulent gardens and pools of water. Today, it is rare to discover an abandoned stone trough along a country lane, as most were long ago claimed by sharp-eyed gardeners and dealers. Stone troughs are now coveted and expensive antiques.

In lieu of antiques, gardeners can purchase newly made stone troughs from skilled masons (it is often nearly impossible to tell the difference between antique or newly made stone troughs), or make or purchase hypertufa troughs. Hypertufa is artificial

A single trough planted with alpines or succulents makes an intriguing accent.

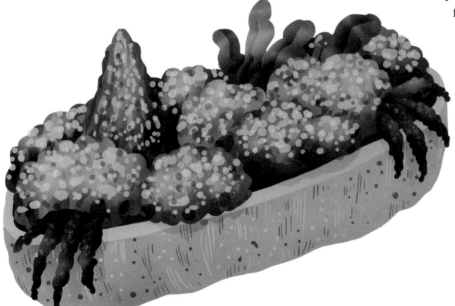

stone made of Portland cement, peat moss, perlite, and water. Hypertufa containers look authentic, have the added benefit of drainage holes, and, with the help of a bit of yogurt (which encourages moss to grow), "age" nicely.

A single trough planted with alpines or succulents makes an intriguing accent. Set in a cottage or country garden, it can look as if it has always been there, once used for livestock. But the acquisition of one trough often leads to more. Troughs are best raised up a bit rather than placed directly on the ground, but a collection massed on a terrace, wall, or table works well and makes a bold statement. Some gardeners give a spacious, graveled area to troughs. One such garden is Thenford Arboretum and Gardens in England, created by the publishers Michael and Anne Heseltine. They have collected more than thirty-eight antique troughs in various shapes and arranged them around the perimeter of what they call their "garden of troughs." In the center is a large circular granite trough from an old cider press.

Tuteur, Obelisk, Pillar

A tuteur, from the French, is a decorative, three-legged support for vines. It evolved from the humble teepee of the vegetable garden. Tuteurs can be made of wood, such as cedar, either unfinished or painted; metal, including copper or steel; or plastic. The sides have plain or fancy cross pieces. Often there is a finial on the top.

A tuteur can be a focal point on its own, punctuating a path, or it can be paired with a second identical tuteur, marking a transition. It can be placed deep in the midst of a bed of flowers, adding height and interest. Most often, tuteurs are graced with lightweight vines such as rose, clematis, or morning glory. But even left unadorned, a tuteur can be a thing of beauty.

An obelisk is a tall, four-sided form, slightly tapered, and topped with a pyramid. The ancient Egyptians were masters of the form and carved massive stone obelisks. Later, the Romans removed some of the Egyptian obelisks, placing them in their own public spaces and even in their gardens. Obelisks were erected in eighteenth-century English landscapes as a way to draw the eye. This was during a time of a rising middle class, the discovery of Pompeii and Herculaneum, and a public fascination with the classical world. Victorian-era Egyptmania, which began after Napoleon's conquest of Egypt, fueled this fascination. In the mid-nineteenth century, that grand American obelisk rising over the capital city, the Washington Monument, was built. Memorial obelisks appeared in American garden cemeteries and in rural graveyards. Having phallic connotations or, as they put it, symbolizing fatherhood, they were usually placed on the graves of men.

Most often, tuteurs are graced with lightweight vines such as rose, clematis, or morning glory.

Today, antique stone obelisks command high prices. Less expensive concrete, composite stone, and occasionally terra-cotta reproductions are available and can be quite beautiful.

Smaller, lightweight obelisks, made of steel, wrought iron, copper, or sometimes wood, are structurally more closely related to the tuteur than to the massive stone monuments of Egypt, but the basic shape remains that of the obelisk. Often, finials or other embellishments replace the pyramid on the top. Airy sides are decorated with curlicues, crosspieces, or other metal work. Like tuteurs, these small obelisks can be placed within the flowerbed itself. Entwined with honeysuckle or other flowering vines, one of these lightweight structures can be a stunning addition to the garden.

Pillars and pillar obelisks are round rather than square or triangular, and have a domed top. Like tuteurs, they have open sides. They are made of metal and sometimes called rose pillars, as roses and clematis are the plants most often grown on them.

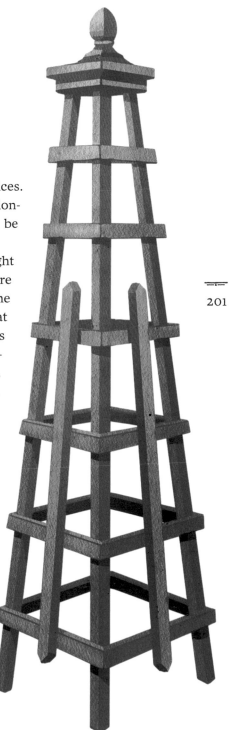

Walled Garden

In 1925, Winston Churchill designed and built a small walled garden, enclosing half an acre. He laid all the bricks himself. Garden historian Jules Hudson believes this is the only walled garden of the many built in England in which the owner did the work of building the wall. This was at a time when walled gardens were being abandoned and falling into ruin. Churchill, however, wanted a place to grow food and share private moments with his friends and family.

Ancient Egyptians, Romans, Chinese, Persians, and Aztecs all walled their gardens from the outside world. Indeed, the notion of garden was a concept of enclosure. Egyptian gardens were walled and attached to the house. The pools, paths, shade trees, potted plants, and quadrants behind the walls ensured that these gardens were a pleasant retreat from the harsh climate of the Nile region. Romans decorated the walls of their gardens with colorful frescoes of birds, flowers, and vines. They included recessed niches for lamps, statuary, and shrines, adding to the ambience. Apparently to ward off thieves, jagged pieces of broken amphorae topped the walls of the kitchen gardens in Pompeii. Romans were also fond of walled sunken gardens, which they made in Pompeii and elsewhere in the empire.

Iran, then known as Persia, was a land of passionate gardeners. It was famous for its walled gardens and parks from the sixth century BCE to the magnificent gardens of Islam. Within the walls, the garden was divided into four quadrants, which themselves might also be divided. *Paradaida*, the Persian word for enclosed garden, is the origin for "paradise" in English.

The Italian Renaissance brought formal walled gardens with skillfully wrought walls, stairs, and terraces. Dazzled, the French, most notably Le Nôtre at Versailles, adopted walled gardens as their own. The Dutch, themselves avid gardeners, followed, creating formal walled gardens in their canaled towns. They were followed by British walled gardens, which remained the fashion until William Kent and Capability Brown banished them in favor of a more natural and parklike landscape. The banishment was not to last. Arts and Crafts designers revived walled gardens, including sunken gardens.

In England, walled gardens were built over a period of 400 years, beginning in the sixteenth century. The walls were made of brick, stone, or cob; brick was the preferred material, for its looks and practicality. Early walls were four or five feet tall, but as horticulture advanced, walls increased in height to accommodate the fruit trees grown against them, reaching as many as fifteen feet or higher. Later walls also sometimes contained stoves and hot air passages, the warmth extending the range and season for the trees. English walled gardens were usually laid out geometrically, typically square or rectangular, but for reasons of terrain and personal taste some were made in odd shapes such as trapezoids and, at William Robinson's Gravetye Manor, an oval. They contained paths, cisterns, fountains, beds and borders of vegetables and flowers, fruit trees, vines and bushes, glasshouses, bothies, privies, cold frames, arbors, pergolas, sheds, and sometimes the head gardener's house. The perimeter outside the wall was also planted.

At first, English walled gardens were attached to or close to the house and might enclose an acre, but once the landscape movement was in sway, walled gardens were destroyed or moved out of site of the manor house, hidden by a shelter belt of trees. These distant walls enclosed many intensely productive acres.

During World War I, men who worked in the gardens were called to the battlefield, where many died. Those who returned were not willing to devote the rest of their days to the smooth functioning of wealthy family estates. Deprived of cheap labor, the gardens were difficult to sustain. Some walled gardens were conscripted for use during World War II, but by the 1960s, most were no longer farmed and fell into rampant overgrowth and ruin. Renewed interest was sparked at the end of the twentieth century, inspired by the highly publicized rediscovery and rejuvenation of the Lost Gardens of Heligan in Cornwall. Other restoration projects ensued.

Leading twentieth century designers—including Gertrude Jekyll, Vita Sackville-West, Beatrix Farrand, David Hicks, and others—created romantic walled gardens in the UK and the United States. Frances Hodgson Burnett immortalized the allure of walled gardens in *The Secret Garden*, published in 1910, now read and beloved by generations of adults and children.

Walled gardens offer a special sense of being apart from the pressures, noise, and bustle of the everyday world. They offer relief from the sun in hot climates and shelter from frigid temperatures in cold climates, protecting plants and people.

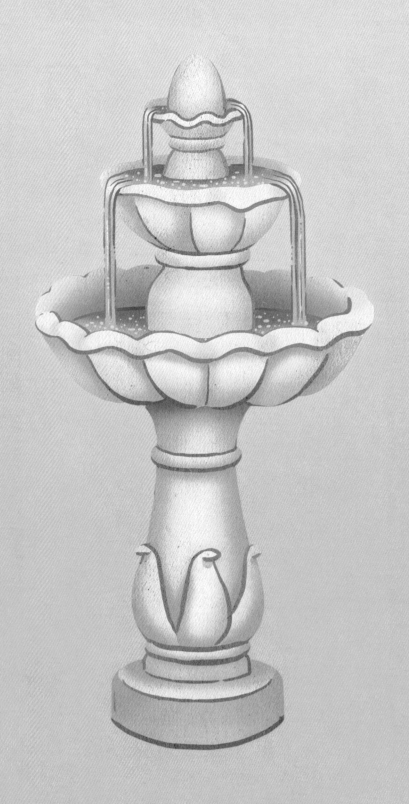

Water Feature

Longwood Gardens in Philadelphia boasts 1719 fountains in its fountain garden—a quintessential example of a water feature. The original 1931 sunken fountain garden was renovated in 2017. The dancing water sprays, one reaching 175 feet in the air, are lit with multicolored LED lights, making for spectacular theater.

The Sun King, Louis XIV, would have appreciated Longwood. His marble, lead, and gilded-lead sculptural fountains—including Apollo, a dragon, dolphins, frogs, and a lion—still spray and flow at Versailles, attracting visitors from afar. Versailles also includes pools and waterfalls. Alas, the king did not have LED lights to add color.

Early fountains were gravity fed. The water source was higher than the fountain. The Romans built aqueducts to carry water to their cities, where lead pipes in turn carried it to homes, gardens, and drinking fountains in city squares. Romans enjoyed a number of water features in their atrium gardens. In addition to fountains, they had cisterns to collect rain water for watering plants. Like the Egyptians and Babylonians before them, they made a decorative feature of the cisterns, which also served as reflective dipping pools. Romans, who enjoyed the company of song birds in their gardens, filled birdbaths for them. Frescoes of the period show gardens filled with flowers, vines, birds, and birdbaths.

Vital for plants to live, water is also an irresistible embellishment.

Cyrus the Great, founder of the First Persian Empire, was an avid and influential gardener. He brought water from distant mountain snowmelt in slanted underground *qanats* or tunnels. Once the water reached his orchards and gardens, it flowed in pretty stone troughs, which were laid out geometrically. Decorative quadripartite gardens with watercourses became the signature layout for Persian gardens for centuries, culminating in the great gardens of Islam still made and admired today.

Where generations of gardeners kept cisterns to collect water for their plants, we might attach rain barrels to our downspouts. Indeed, in most climates, gardeners must ensure a supply of water to sustain plants, employing wells, reservoirs, hoses, drip irrigation systems, and watering cans.

Splish, Splash

In her book, *Come Into the Garden*, Grace Tabor declared that if she could have only one thing in her garden, it would be a birdbath, perhaps the simplest water feature one can add to a garden. Traditional birdbaths consist of a pedestal and a wide, shallow bowl made of terra-cotta or concrete. Situated in an island bed or border, they create a focal point and offer the added benefit of splashing birds to watch. There are hanging birdbaths, birdbaths that contain a solar fountain, and birdbaths with heaters to keep the water from freezing in winter. Artists working in clay, copper, and other materials offer highly original creations.

Vital for plants to live, water is also an irresistible embellishment. Those with enough land might have the good fortune of a natural pond or lake to reflect the clouds in the sky and attract wildlife, or a brook tumbling over mossy rocks. Without such luck, we can create water features ranging from humble to showy, rustic to formal. These can bring the still tranquility of a pool surface or the ripple and energy of a fountain. We can purchase a liner (an impermeable membrane) and, with some excavation, make our own small pond, even a little brook and waterfall, which we can plant with waterlilies and stock with goldfish. If that is not possible, we can fill a lead tank, large livestock tub, even an abandoned clawfoot bathtub with water and plant a few waterlilies. More formally, we can add a stone reflecting pool or rill. The pool can be raised or sunken. If raised, it might have a ledge for sitting. A sunken pool might have a broad edge, or stone steps leading down into it.

The availability of recirculating pumps means anyone can have a fountain in the garden. With a solar-powered pump, one does not even need expensive wiring. The fountain can be purchased ready-made, commissioned from an artist, or contrived from treasured finds, such as an old mill stone for a bubble fountain. It can be freestanding or hung on a wall. A wall fountain, or waterspout, might be a traditional lion's head or gargoyle that spills into a basin below.

Woodland Garden

A woodland garden lush with shade-loving plants such as ferns, astilbes, hostas, and azaleas offers a sense of retreat. A brook or pool, mossy boulders, and a meandering path, perhaps lined with stones or old logs, all add to the peaceful experience. Woodland gardens of this sort were often created during the Country House era in the old forests that lay beyond the formal gardens and pastures of estates. Guests could stroll the paths, enjoy the cool, dappled shade, and escape the afternoon heat. There would be a few rustic benches along the path, and if there was enough wooded land, a glade would open up deep inside the forest.

Italian Renaissance gardens featured woodlands, or *boschi*. The woodland garden of the Villa di Castello, in the hills of central Italy and famous for its fountains, included evergreens, bay laurels, and cypresses. By the sixteenth century, some *boschi* were crossed with straight, axial paths, and might be located within the larger garden as a section rather than around the formal part.

Happily, you can have a woodland garden even without acres of forest. The trees in many suburbs are now mature, shading entire properties. They can then be treated as woodland gardens and underplanted with shade-loving shrubs and perennials. Or, a copse can be created in a portion of a sunny garden, such as a group of white birch surrounded by bulbs and grass. Gertrude Jekyll planted her copse with daffodils, which bloomed before the trees leafed out. In winter, she had woodsmen thin her copse, choosing the interesting bent trees to keep rather than those with straight trunks, a decision that she said baffled the workers. She also used the trees in her copse to provide pea sticks and sturdy stakes, coppicing the Spanish chestnuts every five years.

> Woodland gardens . . . are cultivated gardens, which differ from a forest left wild.

Coppicing and pollarding are two ancient methods of managing trees that open up the woodland to more sunlight for ground covers to flourish and making the trees productive and easy to harvest. Coppicing entails cutting the trees down to "stools" or stumps, so that they resprout with multiple stems. Pollarding entails cutting the top off, leaving a trunk, which sprouts into a head. Coppiced and pollarded trees are in essence kept "forever young," making them resistant to disease and weather events. They can live for hundreds, sometimes thousands of years. Coppiced trees look like shrubs. Pollarded trees look like lollipops and are especially decorative when used to line a walk or avenue.

Woodland gardens offer a wide spectrum of opportunities for the creative gardener, delighting and entertaining both gardener and garden guests. These are cultivated gardens, which differ from a forest left wild. A wild forest is important to our landscape and ecology and offers its own pleasures, but a woodland garden contributes to the well-being of the planet, too, by absorbing carbon dioxide and other pollutants from the atmosphere.

Yard

A yard is the area adjoining a building, such as the front or backyard of a house. The word shares linguistic roots with garden, but in the United States, it may or may not include gardens.

After World War II, as soldiers returned home, married their sweethearts, and started families (the beginning of the Baby Boom), the need for new houses exploded. Developers mass-produced tract houses, covering thousands of acres of what had been agricultural land with identical ranch and Cape Cod starter homes. The typical house came with a lawn planted in the front yard, foundation shrubs such as yew across the front of the house, one or two saplings such as Norway maple that would grow quickly into shade trees, and, in the early years, a small patio in the backyard. In addition, there was typically a short, straight, paved driveway. A straight walk, made of concrete or flagstones, led from the driveway to the front door, which was fronted with concrete steps and wrought iron railings. The front porch, popular since the mid-nineteenth century, was gone. This inexpensive landscaping still influences suburban home development.

Even the simplest landscape changes over time. Many of the homes' original trees died in the first years, and owners replaced them with other species, differentiating one yard from another. Other trees thrived and blocked the sun from much of the front yard. Homeowners added their own touches: a few flower beds, more shrubs, a vegetable garden, swimming pool, or swing set in the backyard, perhaps an addition to the house. Within a decade, many residents of these developments had individualized their properties enough that neighboring homes were no longer identical.

The word shares linguistic roots with "garden," but in the United States, it may or may not include gardens.

Towns passed ordinances and regulations about the maintenance of front yards, including the maximum height of a lawn. In the 1960s, some homeowners began to question the sameness of front yards. They rebelled. They turned their front lawns into wildflower meadows or prairies. Others, yearning for more garden space, planted vegetable gardens in the front, especially if it was the sunniest spot on the property. Flowers and split-rail fences appeared.

In 1982, Rosalind Creasey published *The Complete Book of Edible Landscaping*, which won the Award of Excellence from the Garden Writers of America. A garden designer and restaurant consultant, Creasey had experimented with growing edibles as part of the landscape in the 1970s. Other writers advocated natural landscaping, grandmothers' gardens, and better use of space. Whereas family activities had been confined to the backyard, some designers now advocated for front yards that people could use.

Today, front yards with lawns and foundation plantings are still widespread in suburban and rural America, but the vocabulary has expanded. We see front yards with small terraces, curved walkways, borders, specimen trees and shrubs, sculptures, arbors, gates, and privacy hedges shielding the yard from the street. Today, front yards offer a gracious welcome to guests, a shady spot for a bench or chairs, or a refuge for birds or other small wildlife.

Backyards, which were never as constrained as front yards, now boast outdoor kitchens, decks and patios, pools, potting sheds, pergolas, lawn swings, and garden rooms divided by fences or hedges. The American yard is now often a garden.

Metric Conversions

Length

inches	cm		feet	m
1/4	0.6		1	0.3
1/2	1.0		2	0.6
1	2.5		3	0.9
2	5.0		4	1.2
3	7.5		5	1.5
4	10		6	1.8
5	12		7	2.1
6	15		8	2.4
7	17		9	2.7
8	20		10	3
9	23		12	3.6
10	25		15	4.6
12	30.5		20	6
15	38			
20	50			

Temperatures

$$°C = 5/9 \times (°F - 32)$$
$$°F = (9/5 \times °C) + 32$$

Select Bibliography

Adams, Denise Wiles, and Laura L.S. Burchfield. *American Home Landscapes: A Design Guide to Creating Period Garden Styles*. Portland, OR: Timber Press, 2013.

Anderton, Stephen. *Lives of the Great Gardeners*. New York: Thames and Hudson, 2016.

Anglade, Pierre. *Larousse Gardening and Gardens*. New York: Facts on File, 1992.

Bloom, Alan. *Perennials in Island Beds*. London: Faber and Faber, 1977.

Brickell, Christopher. *The American Horticultural Society Encyclopedia of Gardening*. London: Dorling Kindersley, 1993.

Brookes, John. *The Book of Garden Design*. New York: Macmillan Publishing, 1991.

Brown, Jane. *Sissinghurst: Portrait of a Garden*. New York: Harry N. Abrams, 1990.

Bushnell, Rebecca. *Green Desire: Imagining Early Modern English Gardens*. Ithaca, New York: Cornell University Press, 2003.

Campbell, Susan. *A History of Kitchen Gardening*. London: Frances Lincoln, Ltd., 2005.

Carroll, Maureen. *Earthly Paradises: Ancient Gardens in History and Archaeology*. Oxford: Oxford University Press, 2003.

Cooke, Arthur O. *A Book of Dovecotes*. London: T.N. Foulis Publishers, 1920.

Desmond, Ray. *Kew: The History of the Royal Botanic Gardens*. London: The Harvill Press with the Royal Botanic Gardens, Kew, 1995.

De Wolfe, Elsie. *The House in Good Taste*. New York: The Century Company, 1913.

Drower, George. *Garden of Invention: The Stories of Garden Inventors and Their Inventions*. Guildford, CT: Lyons Press, 2003.

Ely, Helena Rutherfurd. *A Woman's Hardy Garden*. New York: Macmillan Co., 1903.

Evelyn, John. Edited by John E. Ingram. *Elysium Britannicum, or the Royal Gardens*. Philadelphia: University of Pennsylvania Press, 2001.

Farrar, Linda. *Ancient Roman Gardens*. Stroud, UK: Sutton Publishing Limited, 1998.

———. *Gardens and Gardeners of the Ancient World: History, Myth and Archaeology*. Oxford: Oxbow Books, 2016.

Favretti, Rudy J., and Joy P. Favretti. *For Every House a Garden*. Hanover, NH: University Press of New England, 1990.

Festing, Sally. *Gertrude Jekyll*. New York: Viking, 1991.

Fish, Margery. *We Made A Garden*. New York: Modern Library, 2002.

Fisher, Adrian. *Labyrinth: Solving the Riddle of the Maze*. New York: Harmony Books, 1990.

Gothein, Marie Luise Schroeter. *A History of Garden Art in Two Volumes*. Cambridge, UK: Cambridge University Press, 2014.

Hayward, Gordon. *Stone in the Garden: Inspiring Designs and Practical Projects*. New York: W.W. Norton & Company, 2001.

Hedrick, U.P. *A History of Horticulture in America to 1860*. Portland, OR: Timber Press, 1988.

Hentzner, Paul. *Paul Hentzner's Travels in England During the Reign of Queen Elizabeth*. Translated by Richard Bentley, 1797.

Hibberd, Shirley. *Rustic Adornments for Homes of Taste*. Chicago: Trafalger Square, 1987.

Hitching, Claude. *Rock Landscapes: The Pullman Legacy: Rock Gardens, Grottoes, Ferneries, Follies, Fountains and Garden Ornaments*. Woodbridge, UK: Garden Art Press, 2012.

Hobhouse, Penelope. *Penelope Hobhouse's Gardening Through the Ages*. New York: Simon and Schuster, 1992.

Hoyles, Martin. *The Story of Gardening*. London: Journeyman Press, 1991.

Hudson, Jules. *Walled Gardens*. London: National Trust Books, 2018.

Huxley, Anthony. *An Illustrated History of Gardening*. London: Paddington Press, 1978.

Jackson, Hazelle. *Shell Houses and Grottoes*. Princes Risborough, UK: Shire Publications, Ltd., 2001.

Jekyll, Gertrude. *Garden Ornament*. Woodbridge, UK: Antique Collectors' Club, 1982.

———. *Wall and Water Gardens*. New York: Charles Scribner's Sons, 1901.

———. *Wood and Garden, Second Edition*. London: Longmans, Green and Co., 1899.

Jekyll, Gertrude, and Lawrence Weaver. *Gardens for Small Country Houses*. New York: Charles Scribner's Sons, 1914.

Jenkins, Virginia Scott. *The Lawn: A History of an American Obsession*. Washington, DC: Smithsonian Institution Press, 1994.

Johnson, Hugh. *The Principles of Gardening: A Guide to the Art, History, Science and Practice of Gardening*. New York: Simon and Schuster, 1983.

Kyle, Paul, and Georgean Kyle. *Chimney Swift Towers: New Habitat for America's Mysterious Birds, A Construction Guide*. College Station, TX: Texas A&M University Press, 2005.

Laws, Bill. *A History of the Garden in Fifty Tools*. Chicago: University of Chicago Press, 2014.

Lord, Tony. *Best Borders*. New York: Viking, 1995.

Loudon, John Claudius. *An Encyclopaedia of Gardening Comprising the Theory and Practice of Horticulture, Floriculture, Arboriculture, and Landscape Gardening: Including All the Latest Improvements; a General History of Gardening in All Countries; and a Statistical View of Its Present State; with Suggestions for Its Future Progress in the British Isles A New Edition*. London: Longman, Hurst, Rees, Orme, Brown, and Green, 1825.

Morgan, Joan, and Alison Richards. *A Paradise out of a Common Field: The Pleasures and Plenty of the Victorian Garden*. New York: Harper and Row Publishers, 1990.

Morris, Edwin T. *The Gardens of China: History, Art, and Meanings*. New York: Charles Scribner's Sons, 1983.

Mosser, Monique, and Georges Teyssot, eds. *The Architecture of Western Gardens: A Design History from the Renaissance to the Present Day*. Cambridge, MA: MIT Press, 1991.

Plumptre, George. *Garden Ornament: Five Hundred Years of Nature, Art, and Artifice*. New York: Doubleday, 1989.

Repton, Henry. *The Art of Landscape Gardening*. Boston: Houghton Mifflin, 1907.

Robinson, William. *The English Flower Garden and Home Grounds*. London: John Murray, 1833.

Scott, Baillie. *Houses and Gardens*. London: George Newnes Limited, 1906.

Scott, Frank J. *The Art of Beautifying Suburban Home Grounds*, New York: D. Appleton & Company, 1870.

Scott-James, Anne. *The Cottage Garden*. London: Allen Lane, 1981.

Shigemori, Kanto. *Japanese Gardens: Islands of Serenity*. Tokyo: Japan Publications, 1971.

Tabor, Grace. *Come into the Garden*. New York: Macmillan, 1921.

———. *The Landscape Gardening Book*. New York: McBride, Winston, and Company, 1911.

Takei, Jiro, and Marc P. Keane. *Sakuteiki: Visions of the Japanese Garden*, Rutland, VT: Tuttle Publishing, 2008.

Tucker, David M. *Kitchen Gardening in America: A History*. Ames, IA: Iowa State University Press, 1993.

Verey, Rosemary. *Rosemary Verey's Making of a Garden*. New York: Henry Holt and Co., 1991.

Weiss, Allen S. *Zen Landscapes: Perspectives on Japanese Gardens and Ceramics*. London: Reaktion Books Ltd., 2013.

Wilder, Louise Beebe. *Color in My Garden*. New York: Doubleday, Page, and Company, 1918.

Wilkinson, Alix. *The Garden in Ancient Egypt*. London: The Rubicon Press, 1998.

Wood, William. *Wood's New England's Prospect*. Boston: John Wilson and Son, 1865.

Acknowledgments

Spending hours alone with my books and computer to write this, I am deeply grateful to my family and friends who have encouraged and listened throughout the process, most of them gardeners themselves: Gretchen, Dan, and Aaron Geromin, my gardening children; my granddaughters Olivia Geromin, an ardent gardener, and Arielle Geromin, who loves to visit gardens; and my sister Jo Staubach, a passionate gardener. I am also grateful to book and horticultural friends who have given advice and support: Fran Keilty, Nan Sorensen, Carole Horne, David LaPere, Barbara Katz, Bonnie Rose Sullivan, Caragh O'Brien, Karen Grava, Karen Gudmundson, and Ann Shuteran Stetser. Thank you, Roger S. Williams, my valiant agent, and thank you to Tom Fischer, my editor, whose idea began the project, and to Julie Talbot and the rest of the Timber team. And a special thank-you to Joe, who has been in the midst of it all each and every day and never once complained about the stacks of books and papers I scattered throughout the house.

Suzanne Staubach (www.willowtreepottery.us) writes, pots, and gardens in the rural northeastern hills of Connecticut. After a long career in independent bookselling, she has turned her attention full time to her own work. She writes and speaks about garden and ceramic history, and sells her handmade pottery nationwide. Staubach has been an active gardener for decades, with a special interest in garden history.

Staubach has served as President of the New England Booksellers Association, Vice President of the American Booksellers Association, and on the board of the Independent Booksellers Association. In 2008, she was awarded the Lifetime Achievement Award by the Connecticut Center for the Book, an affiliate of the Library of Congress.

Julia Yellow is a Taiwanese illustrator and designer who currently lives and works in Los Angeles. Her clients include the *New York Times, Boston Globe, Washington Post,* and numerous national magazines.